Stay Ahead of the Game

A GUIDEBOOK TO REACHING YOUR MAXIMUM POTENTIAL

Stay Ahead of the Game

A GUIDEBOOK TO REACHING YOUR MAXIMUM POTENTIAL

Arlindo Fernandes

iUniverse, Inc.
Bloomington

A GUIDEBOOK TO REACHING YOUR MAXIMUM POTENTIAL

iUniverse books may be ordered through booksellers or by contacting:

iUniverse
1663 Liberty Drive
Bloomington, IN 47403
www.iuniverse.com
1-800-Authors (1-800-288-4677)

Because of the dynamic nature of the Internet, any web addresses or links contained in this book may have changed since publication and may no longer be valid. The views expressed in this work are solely those of the author and do not necessarily reflect the views of the publisher, and the publisher hereby disclaims any responsibility for them.

Any people depicted in stock imagery provided by Thinkstock are models, and such images are being used for illustrative purposes only.

Certain stock imagery © Thinkstock.

ISBN: 978-1-4759-8999-1 (sc)
ISBN: 978-1-4759-9000-3 (hc)
ISBN: 978-1-4759-9001-0 (e)

Library of Congress Control Number: 2013910809

Printed in the United States of America.

iUniverse rev. date: 6/17/2013

Contents

Introduction

THE CIRCUMSTANCES BY WHICH WE originated don't matter. What matters is that the process evolved with love, care, and desire, all for the purpose of filling the obligation of the mystery of the incomprehensible, while never understanding with certainty how it happened the way it happened or how it will end. What we have some certainty of is that after all was said and done, in the five- to seven-day marathon of many competitors—up to two hundred sperms compete—only the one that penetrates first will fertilize the egg. And that proves that each of us is a winner from the very beginning.

The losers would have been my brothers or sisters, and sadly, they didn't have a chance to go home and prepare for the next marathon, because as far as we know, there is only one chance for them to compete. Maybe if I'd known that was the case, I would have let them win the race. But again, either I was the chosen one, or it was meant to be the way it turned out to be. We don't really know, and we can only know what is allowed for us to know. And that allows me to say that we are beyond complicated. Luckily, we are allowed to understand who we are, where we came from, and what the purpose is of all of us, collectively and individually, before we move to what we don't know—and will never know, it seems, unless one day we are granted permission.

Winning the marathon is the first step of the long, complicated, and mysterious process of transforming a tiny, thick, whitish liquid into something extraordinarily amazing and complicated. There is a time limit for complete development, for which we must wait, to truly become one; otherwise, we are a winner who didn't make the cut. We can't temper with time, even if we wanted to. Seven months, minimum—preferably nine—are necessary to get us ready to experience what we are meant to be. The only thing we can do is hope that everything goes the way it is supposed to go during that period, so we can count as the desired and wished-for ones. I believe that while we impatiently wait, we imagine the world of even greater astonishment. It has to be so wonderful—the true paradise for us to enjoy, from one beginning to the other end. We can almost smell, feel, see, and touch that paradise. We must be special, and what awaits us must match what we are. And as much as we want to break free and begin the new journey in that paradise, the desire of others, especially our moms and dads, is equal to ours, to welcome us to the paradise. We make them look and feel even more special. We give them confidence that they have reached the expected milestone … and beyond. If we are the first one born, the joy of satisfaction is elevated.

Now that we are free, part two of life begins. We are winners, heroes at birth, born for continuity and difference. We carry the torches of hope and prosperity to those before us, for us, and to those after us. Because we are winners—heroes with specialties—much is expected of us, and deliverance becomes our obligation. We receive training, guidance, and support to help us stand on our feet and grasp the necessary means to fulfill the dreams of so many by accomplishment of our mission. Failure is not acceptable. And so, let's begin by understanding the reality that surrounds us, which path to travel, and what our mission truly is. Let's design the best possible road maps to get there faster, safer, and more glorious than those before us have done. We are the ones with great powers. "With great power comes great responsibility."

1

The Game Begins

WE ARE THE BEST THING yet to our parents, relatives, and the world. We receive love and care from everybody. We grow up under this condition, while trying to understand the world in which we are living. We learn about our surroundings through instinct, imitation, and development of self-awareness. Each day is a new day for us. Each day we improve on what we learned yesterday, today, and a moment ago. We accumulate experience as we learn the ways of life.

The more we grow, the more we accumulate. The more we accumulate, the better we become. The better we become, the more we understand. The more we understand, the more we want to understand more.

We feel great when we succeed, sad when we lose, and frustrated when we challenge something we want to dominate. Sometimes we cry; other times we just give up. Most of the time help comes from parents or relatives. We register all that as experience and understanding—sometimes we win, and other times we lose, even with the help. We notice that everybody around us, including Mom and Dad, is happy sometimes, sad other times, and concerned most of the time. Everything is intriguing. We try to work out the puzzle, but we come out short of answers. We tell ourselves, however, that because everybody is in the big mystery, it must be the game of life. We understand the tricks of the game as we grow and continue to play.

When things are explained to us, it all makes sense, and we are happy. Suddenly, we are face-to-face with more mysteries, and we feel lost again, because what was just explained to us doesn't connect anymore. That could be because sometimes, explanations are white lies, given just to make us stop asking questions, so grown-ups can go back to doing something important. Fortunately, we begin to understand better by ourselves, and we realize that life is a game of many tricks, laws, rules, and regulations. We didn't choose to be in the game, but there we are, with everybody as one of our team or our adversary, all playing hard.

Time will come during the game when we will wish not to play—we wish that we wouldn't grow, because we understand that the more we grow, the harder the game is and more is expected from us. We get scared, confused, and want to go home. And if not for the encouragement of teammates (friends and siblings), the love of the coaches (parents), and promises of prizes (life's rewards), we would not play.

Our odds of winning are decided by how well we master the game and how determined we are to dominate the game. By staying ahead of the game, we make the odds look good.

2

Who Are You?

THE ROAD TO KNOWING AND understanding who you are divides into two sections. The first section is about your ancestors; the second is about you. That means you have to know who your ancestors are, identify what changes or modifications happened to the family tree before you arrived, and have a reflection of the reverse trip of your life. Instead of looking at where you're going, you look at where you have been. After that, you put things together and try to understand who you are. Then you can look at where you are and where you're going, and see if you need to make adjustments to stay on course.

To know yourself by ancestry doesn't mean that you have to spend all your money and time searching for your first generation. Begin by observing the normal behavior and acts of your parents, brothers, sisters, uncles, aunts, and cousins. Ask your parents about their parents and their parents' parents. Go as far back as you want, depending on how well you want to know where you came from.

Do this to find out the potential as well as the weakness you inherited, so you can work to improve your natural skills and take advantage of them, as well as work on your natural weakness to find out what you are and can be. You will know the bad and the good that run in the family tree. You will take measures to make the best of your gifts and quarantine the evil. Say your grandparents lived a humble and happy life, and your parents are doing the same. Then you are a person of good heart who can hold love, relationships, and friendship fine. On the other hand, if arguments and endless fights separated your parents, the chances are that you will have some social trouble and turbulent relationships. If your mom was raised on welfare, kids will live on welfare. If your uncle and cousins spent most of their time in trouble with the law and had little education, your future may have a slim chance of not getting in trouble with the law.

After you get all the clues about what you might inherit from your ancestors, move to analyzing your own past behavior to get a better clue of who you are and can be.

By about age five, we are what we will be for life—angel or devil, stupid or genius, assassin or peacekeeper, tyrant or democrat, Russian spy or American best. You get the idea. The true you is visible by the time you are thirteen to nineteen. This is when the devilish phase of human nature—when invincibility and the explosive attitude of a refusal to take orders from your parents and teachers—embraces you and won't let go. Only after this phase passes does your maturity begin to develop, as work, car, lovers, rent, and other life demands kick in. Now your personality begins to take the final shape.

When this happens, it is time for you to soul-search, something you do by yourself for yourself, with benefits to you and others. For many of us, this search for knowing who we are is nothing more than a waste of time, because we are not taught about its importance as we grow up. Like many other important things in life, we are left to decide if we want or need to know who we are. If we learn about who we are and who we can be, we could block so many bad things that will come to us. We could have a better understanding of where to go, where not to go, and to whom we should stay close or keep apart from.

Say you have a hot temper. If you understand that you have a hot temper, you will know that the way for you to stay free from trouble is to avoid confrontation with others who also have hot tempers. You also will stay away from violent video games and watching TV shows like Jerry

Springer's and the like. You will avoid listening to music dominated by hateful lyrics and will avoid chaotic situations, because you know that you have a bad temper, and those aspects of life will make your personality worse.

Instead, you look for people with peace in their hearts to be your friends; practice a religion with a doctrine of love, peace, and goodwill; exercise and practice yoga; become a Scout; volunteer for a charity; and so on. And of course, get an education and a high social position.

Finding out who you are will save you from spending time in prison. You might be given a break on your first misdemeanor, but you will be slapped hard if you commit felonies and will lose your freedom if you commit murder or other gruesome crimes. And you can't blame the judicial system, because it is your responsibility to know about your natural condition that makes it difficult for you to obey the law with regard to the safety of others and stay away from criminal behaviors.

It's so sad that many young, powerful lives are lost—locked up for a time or for life, or even on death row—because these individuals didn't know who they were; they didn't know they inherited criminal tendencies. If they had known, they could have received help before tragedy struck.

But the troubles that come from knowing who you are is not with the law only. It is with everything you do. Years ago, a friend of mine had a job where one employee, David, was weird-looking and hard to get along with. One day, my friend's coworker complained to the supervisor that he didn't feel safe working with David because he'd seen David angrily punching a trailer and throwing stuff. David was fired, and it was only later that they found out he'd been acting that way because his girlfriend had a miscarriage. A year later, another employee was fired because he threw a chair in the cafeteria and dented the wall—this wasn't his first incident of this kind. His friends commented that he was making good money and really needed that job, but his attitude and behavior got him in trouble and fired. There also are cases of employees being fired for insubordination, fights with coworkers, or punching supervisors.

An uncontrolled temper can cause social disintegration too. You might get into fights at nightclubs, have road rage, argue with your neighbors, and worst of all, go through hell in personal relationships. Restraining orders might keep you away from your ex, and the new partners will leave you as soon they find out about your temper. These bad things could happen because you don't know who you are; you don't see the need to change yourself. Sadly, this bad aspect of life generally targets the poor and uneducated. Rich, educated people have the intellectual capability to see what their kids can be, and they have the economic power to turn their kids into successful individuals. When parents don't have the capability to see what their kids can be and guide them in the right direction, the only support the kids have is education. Education does not eradicate bad behaviors, but it gives kids the power to understand the importance of thinking before they act. With time, this principle will become part of what guides their normal behavior.

If your parents couldn't provide you with a good education, it becomes your responsibility to give it to yourself. Remember your cousin Vinny and his high school dropout dogs on the streets? They were just chilling with drugs, guns, and "bitches" and all were on probation. Then Vinny decided to follow his uncle's advice to get off the streets and go back to school. Do you know who he is now? He's the manager of a shoe distribution center. And his buddies? Some are still on the streets or are in prison, and the rest are homeless, with criminal records a mile long.

There's no greater weapon to fighting all the wars in life than education. It prepares you to face whatever lies ahead with confidence and certainty of achievement. No matter how bad your temper is, when you get yourself to the level of a chief executive officer of a large company, your bad temper has no chance of survival.

Everywhere you go, education rules. My grandma used to tell me that education was the key that opens all doors. Eventually, that philosophy sank in and stayed with me. It made me the man that I am—and I like myself. I like myself a lot. My brothers and sisters have great personalities, and they love themselves too, and we all love each other. Love runs freely in this family, and I made myself even better by stretching higher through education.

Let's all praise education, because it shapes us to be the best we can be. Human complexity and personality uniqueness make it impossible for us to fully understand and control ourselves, but we have the power and means to embrace what is good and stay away from what is bad. We should make the effort to know ourselves to the best of our ability so we can avoid walking blind and coming out with a bleeding nose and a cut on the forehead. It's never too late to find out who you are and make necessary adjustments.

3

Education

Traits that separate us from other animals include the ability to stand upright, walk on two feet, and talk, as well as the intelligence that allows us to build things, cook meals, use utensils, read, write, and communicate verbally. But these abilities must be developed and put to work for maximum results. Education is one of the best ways to do that.

We divide our education process in three ways: home education, school education, and self-education. Home education is the mainframe of our personality for life—the foundation of our success or the roots of our failure. During our first five years, we absorb every experience that happens in our home. We copy the behavior around us, with its tradition, culture, and philosophy. If love, care, respect, and intellect surrounds our home, that's pretty much what we will display when we grow up. On the other hand, if everybody around us is arguing and fighting, or if illiteracy dominates the family, chances are we will have problems shaping our life to the path of love, care, and success.

You don't have control over your home education. The only option you have is waiting until you can take your destiny in your hands and shape your surroundings in a way that you like better, or move out to pursue your dreams, away from negative home experiences and forces.

School education is the greatest gift you will ever have. It will prepare you for the journey that lies ahead by teaching you the basics of this universe, a critical thinking process, and an intelligent way of life, which open the doors for continuing brain development and thinking processes.

School education is affected, however, by home education. If your family is educated, they will prioritize your school education, because they understand its values, now and forever. But if no one in the family passed second grade, you could stay on the same level or lower. And again, you can only change things around when you are able to make decisions for your life. Take education as the most important tool to shape your future. From here, you move on with self-education. That also can happen when your education has reached the level beyond learning from anybody. With critical thinking, you make observations, apply what you have learned, and come up with the conclusion. You will constantly read books and magazines and watch educational television programs to enrich your self-education. It is such a great gift that our generation is blessed with abundant information and the possibilities to help us become whatever we want to become.

Education of any kind is what you must have in order to succeed in life. Then you are protected by reinforcement against the dangers of ignorance and stupidity. We all have heard parents say that they sacrifice so their kids can have a better life than theirs. They make sure their kids get good education, but that is not enough. We must earn the supplemental education for ourselves. It doesn't matter how far along you are in your education; you must use all possibilities and opportunities to improve your education.

I still remember that every time I had a tantrum in my teenage years, my grandmother would remind me that "education is the key that opens all the doors." The beauty of education is that it serves you even when you don't notice. Alternately, the lack of education hurts you every day.

There is not a single aspect of life in which education diminishes your chances of accomplishment or increases the odds for your failure. Only the opposite happens. Jails are filled with inmates of low or no education. Those in trouble with the law; who have trouble in their friendships, relationships, or workplace; or who are involved with drugs, alcohol abuse, or prostitution are the ones with low or no education. Only education can eradicate the forces that stop us from advancing in life and give us the necessary tools to overcome obstacles. Only education can vanquish the human savageness in us and shape our personality to something powerful, desirable, responsible, productive, and intelligent.

Until you get a good education, you are a cursed failure, doomed to hell. With the world and humanity going insane, governments lost, and politics confused, education is the only medicine to cure the illness and help you understand, cope, and take your destiny in your hands. You must stay ahead of the game. If you think you don't need the support of the power of education, you are truly kidding yourself and falling fast behind the game. Get a good education and create better conditions for everybody. This is the only way we count. This is a must.

4

The Chain Reaction

Do you know what happens to factories when the assembly lines are down? The production stops. If there is a back-up plan, it covers the downed lines to keep the employees busy while the lines are being repaired. If the repair is not a quick fix, employees will go home for the day. A too-wet spring hurts farming. A longer, colder winter with frequent storms and blizzards will cause city budgets to shrink fast. If there's a hotter-than-usual summer with drought, farming will be hurt, the harvest will be below normal, and the government will have to increase subsidies to farmers—and then grocery prices will go up. Wildfires destroy properties and leave people homeless. When nations go to war, gas prices go up. Delivering goods and services costs more, and prices go up at the pump. Groceries cost more, and employers freeze hiring and withhold promotions. Employees are asked to do more, but their paychecks don't cover their expenses. People are more frustrated, road rage increases, and accidents are more frequent. The Safe Driver insurance plan points go up, and there's more frustration, because everything is connected to everything, one way or another.

Do you know what happens when assembly lines do not operate efficiently? The productivity is less than standard. The factory will not meet its bottom line, there will be no profits, and layoffs could take place.

This could be followed by bankruptcy to protect the owners, which will send employees to the unemployment line. To avoid this, maintenance of assembly lines should be a top priority.

Let's take the example of a car. There are hundreds of things that must work right on a car so that it can do what it is designed to do. To start the car, we need the key, starter, battery, electrical wires, relays, fuses, ignition, ignition coil, spark plugs, injectors, gas, fuel pump, fuel lines (feed and return), and air.

To keep the engine running, we need all engine components (cylinders, valves, cam shaft, timing belt, timing belt tensioner, water pump, and oil pump), alternator/battery, and the engine's accessories (belts, radiator, fan, radiator hoses, and coolant).

To get the car rolling, we need to have a steering wheel, steering column, rack and pinion, spindle, drive shafts, and transmission; to stop the car we need a brake paddle, master cylinder, brake fluid, brake lines, brake hoses, rotors, brake pads and/or drums, wheel cylinder, and brake pads and shoes.

For transportation, the car must have all that I described, plus a valid safety inspection sticker that includes the inspection of suspension components (control arms, ball joints, tie rod, tie rod end, sway bar, sway bar links, shocks, struts), body damages, driver's side mirror, rearview mirror, headlights, directionals, emergency brakes, and windshield. There are also the little things that are not mandatory to inspection but still important, such as bushings, boots, and mounts for a smooth ride. And last but not least are all the lug nuts, screws, and electronics that must all work in harmony for us to have a reliable car.

You get the idea of the car's chain reaction. Do you know what happens when any of the parts or components don't work properly?

Depending on the nature of malfunction, the car might not start, or it could provide a bumpy ride or even a fatal crash. The secret to avoiding all that is making sure that the car maintenance gets the attention it deserves and the repairs are done in time. We often pay extra for repairs because we wait until things get really bad and then go to the garage. We find out that more things are damaged because we kept driving a sick car. You should know that the smaller and simpler the car, the easier and cheaper the repair and the maintenance. Whatever you drive, however, follow your manual and recommendation, and fix the car as soon something needs repair. It will avoid your being stranded or dead on the road—and you'll save a buck or two.

The chain reaction of a car and human are similar and require just about the same kind of attention. For example, when you have a simple lifestyle—you live with your parents, you have a small school loan, you walk or carpool to work, and you have no or small credit card debt—your chain reaction is small and easy to keep your life running smoothly.

In a medium lifestyle—where you have a good job, a decent salary, car on the road, rent, a small student loan, and your credit cards are in good shape—your chain reaction is neither simple nor difficult, and its running and maintenance don't give you headaches.

As you move up on the ladder of life, things become more complicated as the chain extends and sophisticates. Trouble can come at any time from all directions, and when it does, you'd better be prepared!

Say you are in your thirties with a family and home of your own. You have a decent job and are climbing the corporate ladder. Maybe you'll never be president, chief executive officer, or chief financial officer, but you can reach a high level. Your mortgage is affordable, your spouse contributes to your annual household expenses, and your credit score is good. You are living the American dream!

In this case, your chain looks like this: property taxes; mortgage; house liabilities; maintenance of gutters, plumbing, heating, and electricity; cable and phone bills; house renovation, driveway, and lawn care; dog food and vet visits; kids' entertainment and after-school programs (karate, dancing, piano lessons); and car payments, insurance, gas, and repairs. You also could be hanging around with the big boys from the office, playing golf on weekends, and there are expenses related to that sport.

As you can see, the larger your life is, the more complicated and demanding your chain reaction becomes. The maintenance of your chain reaction requires you to stay on top of the most important parts of the chain first. That means pay your mortgage or face foreclosure; pay your car payments or ride on the bus; pay your insurance premium or lose your insurance; be late to work, call in sick frequently, perform below standards consistently, and see yourself on the unemployment line. These important parts get our attention by nature. We naturally care about them. Smaller parts—car repair, credit card payments, hospital bills, and other small financial compromises—get less attention, as they don't disrupt the chain reaction as radically.

The less important ones, such as small loan payments to a friend, tire rotation, and savings and retirements funds are parts of the chain that usually come last on the priority list. Then there's the mentality of "if it's not broken, don't fix it." But the danger of bringing that kind of approach into the chain reaction of your life is that you will wait until your chain breaks to fix it, instead of taking care of it and making repairs before it breaks.

The wise thing to do is to divide attention among all components, big and small, of the chain and make small adjustments before things get out of hand, especially on your complex chain reaction—when it breaks, you may never be able to repair it. This principle works the same way in real life. When you neglect making that sixty-dollar payment to a friend, school loan, or insurance, and use the cash on unnecessary purchases, telling yourself that you will take care of business next month, you not only increase your next month's expenses but also put yourself on troublesome roads. When you are late on your mortgage and car payments, you increase your financial burden and damage your credit. So here is the catch: if one section of the chain of your life works poorly, it is not so disturbing; if five sections work poorly, the chain reaction is definitely problematic.

To avoid this road, monitor your assembly line every day. Fix the parts that are about to break, or correct what doesn't look right. When you get the chain working smoothly, don't sit down, relax, have a drink, and play video games. For your chain reaction to work smoothly, you must have the determination to do your part—and do it right. That's how you stay ahead of the game. Some of us begin the chain reaction with a smooth flow and others gradually bring it there, but most of us are still working on it. The main point is to focus on maintenance after you have your chain reaction working as it should be working. When you see a tire about to go bald, or the alignment on your car about to go bad, take care of it. Don't wait until the tires explode on the highway or drive your car when it's out of alignment. That's not staying ahead of the game. Understand the chain reaction of your life, be aware of it, and keep a close eye on it. Take necessary measures as soon you see the need. That's how you stay ahead of the game.

5

The Government

YOU CAN RUN, BUT YOU can't hide. No matter how badly you want the government to go away, it will stick around until the end of the time. You can blame it for all the tragedies in your life, but it is not going anywhere. It is the evil we can't live with and we can't live without. It is the necessary devil to guide and guard our destiny!

Our barbaric behavior made it necessary for someone to stand up to established order in the house. That indicates that first it was us, and then there was the government. In an attempt to do something fair and square for everybody, the government created laws, rules, and regulations for us to obey. But our behavior became wilder and more disrespectful, the government's work became more complex, the measures to keep us in line became increasingly harsher, and the chaos never slowed down.

The whining and more whining of people from the north, south, east, and west and left and right makes the government ignore the whining even more, because it would go deaf trying to listen to everybody. While trying its best, the government is always behind the game, it seems.

Every nation's laws are written by the finest heads, submitted to the finest of finest heads for review, and are close to perfect before they are approved. They are often written in a way that the common man can't understand, so the big shots can make a buck or two translating it for us and representing us in front of a judge—and this may seem unfair, but it's necessary. It's necessary for reasons that we don't understand—we don't have what it takes to understand. Maybe we shouldn't worry, because everything the government does is in attempt to be fair and square to everyone.

Government is like a hardworking family, where the president is the chief of the household, with many uncounted children. Brothers, sisters, uncles, cousins, aunts, grandmothers, grandfathers, landscapers, housekeepers, and drivers—the government branches—all work together to help the chief of the household take care of the family, give unconditional love to all, and protect the children from strangers. On top of that, there's taking care of the illegitimate kids kept under the radar. Oh yes, the burden of the government's responsibility is light by no means. Let's touch just some of the issues it has to deal with when reality strikes.

When tornadoes, hurricanes, floods, and earthquakes strike, the government is there to protect, rescue, relocate, shelter, and rebuild. When flu, mad cow disease, and EEE (eastern equine encephalitis) attack, the government takes measures to protect us and takes preventive measures to avoid epidemics and pandemics. It requires that people coming here are disease-free and makes children's vaccinations mandatory. It protects our skies, waters, and land from national and international enemies, alien invasion, and Communist takeover; protects us from extinction; and spies on and chases all spies. It's the government that patrols our streets twenty-four/seven, so we can have tranquil nights of sleep and keep our belongings. And if you happen to be the victim of a robbery or other crime, the government provides qualified people to track down the perpetrator and bring him to justice. When we go to the jungle and forget our way back to civilization, the government releases cops and K-9s, helicopters, and the National Guard for search and rescue. It also sends divers to the bottom of lakes to find us or sends fire trucks and ambulances to the scene to take us to the best medical facility, regardless of our color, race, gender, or religion. When we travel abroad, the government makes sure that we are going to a safe place. If something goes wrong, the government finds out what happened so justice can be served and prevents the same bad things from happening to others. The government created the World Trade Organization, international treaties, and special economic relationships to ensure fair business all around the world. It monitors inflation so we don't lose too much when we go to Best Buy, Walmart, or Home Depot. The government takes care of the beauty of our landscape—lakes, ponds, and parks—and architecture of our towns and cities. It protects us from water and food contamination and ensures that the food and drugs we deal with don't kill us. The government protects us from Russian missiles and from cyber and biological attacks. It maintains a military superpower, so no one messes with the United States. The government takes care of national security to make sure that when guests come here, they are what they claim to be.

I truly believe that the government deserves more credit than it gets.

Mad Society

Some say, "You must be brain-dead, high, and on drugs to praise the government. We know that everything that the government puts its hands on turns out a deadly failure." Every day, taxpayers want to choke the government because of the lies, corruption, cover-ups, unnecessary bureaucracy, and luxury and overspending, just to mention a few bad behaviors. The rich and very rich, now said to be 1 percent of the population, are angry about policies that prevent them from taking over. The middle class, now said to be 99 percent of the population, is angry because their dreams are being shattered as government cuts their potential to thrive by sucking up their dollars on taxes and fees. And the poor and very poor people still exist. The middle class has been erased! Why did Romney say that he doesn't worry about the 47 percent—the poor who do not pay taxes? That means 52 percent of us are middle class, right? Besides, both he and President Obama were talking about making things better for the middle class, because the poor are protected by a safety net. As long as you stay poor, you are fine, and the rich are always fine.

In reality, society is divided into three classes: rich, middle, and poor. There is a small number in the rich class, a good number in the middle class, and the largest number in the poor class—and all three classes need to do better. This has been shown through Occupy Wall Street and the like worldwide, mainly by the middle class. And if we are going to the streets worldwide, it's because we are really fed up, Government. We might have run out of good advice, but we are telling you that you'd better get your act together. You are pushing us back into poverty, you are destroying the generation, you are killing the essence of the middle class, and you are defeating the purpose of the pursuit of happiness.

We appreciate the good that you do, and we forgive you for the errors you commit. We are angry at the mistakes you make and that you leave doors open for more. We know that you can do better. And for that, yes, we are angry—very angry.

Middle Class

Here is where the party lives—the excitement of living the American dream at its core and turning dreams into reality. The good, the bad, and the ugly and friends, enemies, and families all gather in the middle class. This segment of society is where all four seasons of the year dance merrily and harshly—merry most of the time but very harsh sometimes.

Neither painful like the bottom, nor as stressful as the top, it is perfect for excitement. In this class, you will find people with advanced education, good-paying jobs, nice homes and yards with in-ground swimming pools, and friendly neighbors. The beautiful wife and smart, handsome husband have one daughter, two sons, and a dog. The businessman has a good nine-to-five job, Monday through Friday, and is the generator of the main income. The middle class knows Friday is for the club, Saturday is for shopping, and Sunday is for church and friends. They take cruises and overseas travels for vacations once a year. The middle class just rocks! It is so true that President Obama and Governor Romney both focused their concern on the middle class during the 2012 presidential "war." Who wouldn't want to belong to the middle class? Not me!

This appealing lifestyle comes with a price tag, however, to keep the happiness standing strong. That price tag includes items that require maximum attention, such as education, employment, finances, society, and family. Usually, these items are under control. Whenever something goes off track, immediate measures are taken, and everything is back to normal. But every time the world goes on its uncontrollable economic downward spiral, the middle class takes the knock-out punch, because it has so many sections of the assembly line that we must take care of in all economic weather conditions. Let's see what and why.

School loan: You must repay. Most school loans come from private lenders who are likely not to give you a break. Government loans could give some breaks for hardship when you qualify, but you shouldn't count on it.

Mortgage: If your mortgage is variable, count on its being higher than previous months. And if your tenants don't pay rent, you still must pay your mortgage to the bank.

Finance: You could find yourself unemployed, relying on 60 percent of your previous pay and the salary of your spouse. Chances are, both incomes combined will not cover all your main financial responsibilities, and the secondary responsibilities, such as soccer, music classes, and after-school programs, will be in jeopardy too. The only thing that could come to your rescue is your savings—something that nobody likes to touch—and your credit cards.

Your behavior: The last thing you want to do is get in trouble. You know that you need to stay a law-abiding citizen. The problem is that when you are under a lot of pressure, you could easily get in an argument with your spouse, get in your car, and run a red light. Or you might be so involved with thinking about your problems that you rear-end another car. There is also the possibility that stress will push you to say things unintentionally, and you will get a warning at your work and hurt your chances of a promotion or good raise. You know that as a member of the middle class, there are eyes on you all the time. Your behavior and social appearance are always watched.

Job security: To keep a competitive edge over your coworkers and newcomers, you must keep your skills upgraded through evening courses at your local community college and online courses.

The helping hand: The government loves you. At times, you wish it didn't, but it does. The government knows that things can turn sour for the middle class. For that, it allows you to have a share of the assistance that is for the poor. Except that you, as a middle-class individual who is desperately in need of a little help until the storm passes, will not qualify for assistance. You must fall in the net so that you can legally get protection. Your friends in the safety net know all the back doors, and they are always willing to show you the way—that's a chance for them to show their appreciation for the favors and support you give them. The only problem is that getting the support through the back door will complicate your life if you get caught. Actually, you don't dare to take any chances because you know that your social security number is the mirror that shows the government your face, as well as the places you have been and the history of your actions. All the chains of your assembly line are connected to your social security number. One single distorted link gets the whole assembly line in trouble.

Anyone in the safety net can get behind the wheel and drive anywhere without license and registration. If caught, he or she may face arrest, a court date, and maybe a fine. If that person gets a loan or buys on credit, he can default on those payments and not care, because he doesn't have much to lose if legal actions are taken. The worst that can happen is jail time. But if you, the middle class individual, get in that car and drive it without license and registration, and you get caught, you are pretty much dead. And if you default on your financial obligations to the lenders and companies that provide services for you, you have much to lose, because you will mess up your whole assembly of life. Of course, it is unfair that people in the safety net get away with it, and you don't. Doesn't this explain why they say life is not fair?

Government expects you to perform flawlessly or else. You have to protect your credit score, because you don't know when you are going to need a refinance for house repairs, replacement of the heating system, or an emergency loan of some kind. Keeping your credit score in good standing will save you money, as you get a lower interest rate. And it will save you the hassle of having to find a co-signer. For that, you must play by the rules with the cards that you have.

Maintaining the life standard is difficult, even impossible at times. A bad economy pushes you down, and you can't find anything to grab onto as you fall fast, so you take desperate measures. The stress and frustration mounts, and the rage against the government becomes impossible to suppress.

It just sucks that you are so important for the government, but when things go bad due to factors that are beyond your control, you are on your own. The worst of all is that you see and smell the waste right in front of your nose, and you sense the government's nonsense in philosophical principles. If it is expected that the government helps those in need, it is only fair that you get help when you need it.

But you should not curse the government and put your guard down just because we are doomed. Even when the government is the one to blame, take each swing of life as a positive experience, and hold on tightly as you move to the next, better thing. You may see yourself close to the safety net, but you are not there yet, and you know that you don't belong there. In fact, you are the one keeping the safety net alive. Fair or not, you must fight the hard times and move your position to higher class only. So hang on strong, adjust your priorities, and hold big dreams and projects until the storm quiets down. It always does. Then it will be full speed ahead again. Remember that you are not the only class that dislikes the government. Occupy Wall Street was a worldwide thing. Take your destiny in your hands, respect what the government wants you to respect, use whatever it has available for your benefit, and stay away from what seems legal but smells fishy. Don't waste your time trying to understand why the government seems so stupid. Instead, use your brain to figure ways for your success.

Your Driver's License

You probably couldn't wait to get your driver's license. You knew that it was the legal document that would put you behind the wheel and take you wherever you wanted to go. Well, let me tell you something: Your driver's license is much more important than you think. It comes to you as paradise or hell, depending on how you care for it. The same government that gave it to you can take it away from you, temporarily or forever, and leave you stranded, looking toward a very sour journey. All your protectors are now like wild dogs unleashed. Make one wrong move, and watch yourself bleeding from a wild dog bite. You must exercise maximum caution, and use your brain and common sense, because you are at war with the government. To win the war, you need to follow the laws, rules, and regulations of the government. And so, let's look at ways to avoid the madness.

Address change: Inform the Department of Motor Vehicles (DMV) of your new address every time you move to a permanent address. Why? Because the DMV could send you notification about suspension of your license to your old address. I once found out after doing something stupid—I flew through a tollbooth without paying the fee—that the violation ticket was sent to the address connected to my license plate. If that had happened to be an old address, I would not have received the ticket. Penalties would have mounted until I went to renew my license, and I'd have found out there were a thousand dollars in outstanding charges. No payment, no renewal.

Excise taxes: Pay your excise taxes on time, all the time, especially at times when you will soon renew your license or register a car. Also remember to

- pay all your driving violations on time;
- pay all your parking tickets on time, all the time;
- renew your plates on time; and
- renew your driver's license on time.

Other important tips to remember:

- Never drive without your license. When you have no other option, make sure you exercise maximum caution, and be prepared to face the consequences in case you're stopped.

- Don't drive any uninsured car; you will face impounding, arrest, jail, and court.
- Don't drive drunk—period.
- Don't ever drive with a suspended license. That could spell jail. Double the trouble when both the car and you are unlawfully on the road. When you are illegally on the road, the cops will lock you up and impound your car. Towing and storage fees will be your responsibility. Caution, common sense, and respect for the laws and regulations of driving will save you a lot of trouble.
- Never cross double yellow lines.
- Never violate driving rules just because you don't see cops around; detectives and cops may be camouflaged in station wagons, BMWs, and SUVs.
- Never park in a handicapped parking spot.

Circumstance: There are times when emergency strikes, leaving us without a way to comply with laws and regulations. For example, your car won't start, and you must be somewhere important. Then you have to borrow your friend's car. You are not listed on his/her policy as a driver, meaning that legally, you can't drive that car. Since this is an emergency, you are doing wrong for the right reason.

It's your ultimate responsibility to avoid being in trouble and avoid getting your friend in trouble, so in this situation, you should

- drive at the speed limit (you should do that all the time anyway);
- maintain better than fair distance from the car in front of you, and monitor the cars behind you more frequently than usual;
- stop at all yellow lights, make a full stop at all stop signs, give up the right of way when necessary, and use your directional signals for each turn;
- stay off the fast lane, and be aware of the traffic all around you (avoid vision obstruction by trailers and other vehicles taller than yours);

- be alert to reckless drivers by staying ahead of the game;
- make sure you don't drive the wrong way on a one-way street; and
- park legally (don't double park or park in a handicapped-accessible spot).

This is some precautionary advice, but you should learn about all things that could jeopardize your keeping your license. I advise you to stay current with driving laws, rules, and regulations. I strongly recommend that you stay off the road any time you cannot legally drive.

You are young. We welcome you into the world of the middle class. We need your power and good behavior to stop the fall into poverty. We can't count much on the government. We all want you to stay with us, thrive with us, and give us new ideas. We will show you the good tricks, and together we will take the middle class to where it was before this economic chaos and make it even better. Our wisdom and experience, combined with your power and fresh ideas, are the main generators of the middle class. We are not going to change the government, because we can't; we are going to take charge of our destiny and make the middle class shine again, because we can.

6

The Teenage Years

WHEN YOU'RE A TEENAGER, NO one expects you to stay the same or become a better angel, but no one expects you to turn into an uncontrollable devil either. Unfortunately, turning into an uncontrollable devil is exactly what will happen to you as a teenager, especially the first three years or so. It seems that now life begins talking to us like nobody else does, as we go through so many changes—physical, mental, and emotional.

As teenagers, life talks to us in three stages. The first stage, from thirteen to seventeen, is the one where the most dramatic changes take place. The next stage is age eighteen—the stage we can't wait for. And the third stage is when we become an adult—a young adult, but that matters not, because now those teenage years are history. Freedom has knocked, and we just opened the doors. There's no more calling Mom and Daddy to sign everything for us, and many driving restrictions are lifted.

With the exception of the girls in some cultures, where "sweet sixteen" is the official mark for opening the gates of sex, the sneaky sexual adventures are now in the open—no more ducking, no more "hurry up before Mom comes." As long you keep some respect and decency, Mom and Daddy will leave you alone, for the most part. Now your only concern is avoiding underage girls and teen pregnancy.

Girls are no longer Daddy's little girls. Now they turn to Mom for advice on how to deal with the opposite sex. Daddy is still important, of course, but more for emergency cash than advice and emotional comfort.

You could be moving to college or getting a job. (Don't forget, though, that you need higher education to reach the stars.) Good-bye to fake IDs for nightclubs, strip clubs, liquor, and cigarettes. Freedom is here; party time is here; life is good! But the good time passes fast. In no time, age twenty is here, and that puts you just a year shy of the big one—twenty-one!

When we turn twenty-one, we are full-blooded adults—no more junior things or "young adult" title. We now play with the big boys. At age twenty-one, however, most of us still think and act like teens, except now we pay as adults for the consequences of a teen's thinking and behavior. We are treated as adults, expected to act like adults, and we will be punished like adults. But we have nothing to worry about if we have not messed up previously and our record is clean.

There is the other side of the coin, however, where things have never been smooth, and that needs to change. Maybe you weren't lucky to have a daddy at home, unlike most of your friends. And your mom didn't understand you. Destiny didn't give you a chance to make it to twenty-one without a long criminal record or an undesired child from a casual sexual encounter. It could be that the future looks very foggy for you. You could find yourself talking desperately to yourself. You see yourself not moving at all. The thing that looks doable now is to embrace life at its lowest standards. You try to get a low-paying job at Walmart or Family Dollar, and you keep your fingers crossed that the cops get off your back. Ghetto is what you are; ghetto is what you will be for the rest of your life. Yes, this is a very frustrating situation, made worse by self-destructive thoughts, but you have the power and resources to change things around.

Girls, the government takes care of you at no cost, as long you give it a few healthy babies. But you can choose a better way. Start from scratch, doing it right this time.

Boys, you can do the same. You can still make it. Gear yourself with tigers' strength and go get it. Erase the times that you disrespected your mom, asked your father to fight you, told your teachers to go suck on a big one, or called your sister a bitch and told her to go to hell. That time is past now. Look straight ahead, take a deep breath, and move in the direction of the new, successful you.

Making Dreams Come True

Lucky people are those who have almost everything working for them. They have great personalities, family support, money, and education. They are successful in transforming their dreams into reality. Of course, extra effort doesn't hurt, as it increases the chances and dimension of their dreams, opening new horizons. As long as they don't become lazy, all their dreams will come true in time.

The rest of us, the unfortunate ones, could have some empowerment or no empowerment at all. The one thing that makes us successful is the desire to make it. That desire is what pushes us beyond the wish of making it to turning it into reality. It's that desire that brings pain and suffering to your soul unless you are doing something to satisfy it. It's that desire that makes you walk through trenches and take falls and beatings but keep on going strong. You know that nothing can stop you. You are stronger than anything standing in your way. That's the desire. That desire is spelled "pride within." It is yours and yours alone. Not all of us let it fly free because it's painful, but you are not going to hold yours and take it to the grave. You are going to free it and make it grow. Let it be what it is meant to be, and be an inspiration to others who are afraid of setting their desires free.

The teenage years can be some of the most difficult in human developments, but then along comes all kinds of power to spring us to new heights. We can use those powers to bring out our pride and give us the edge we need to turn our pride into something brilliant. The hardest part is fighting the issues we face that impede us from using our power in a more productive way. But again, there is not a single issue troubling you that can't be taken care of. Your parents are the best people to reach out to, and home is the best place for starting your journey of becoming the star that you are.

7

Friends

MILLIONS OF YEARS AGO, THE organisms that gave us human identity had friends—many, many friends. The fight for survival could only be won with the help of friends.

After evolution reached the thinking level, humans put themselves on the move, and things took a turn—some good, others bad. Once upon a time one of them saw another, who was dragging dead prey, being attacked by the mother, brother, and sisters. He instantly helped the other to win the fight. The prey's family went their way, as losers. The hunters smiled at each other and went their separate ways. The next day they were hunting together; no one needed help, but there was an opportunity to return a favor. A hunting weapon was given as a gift. The day after, both brought company, and a small circle of friends was born. The guy on the other side of the river was watching and liked what he saw but couldn't come over—he didn't know how to swim! And so he created his friends on the other side of the river. Soon after, there were bunch of tribes everywhere. And the rest is history!

As God noticed that Adam was lonely, He gave him Eve to not only end his loneliness but also to reproduce and fill the world with love and brotherhood. I learned that when I was a kid. Sometimes I wonder if God has seen what He's been seeing and fears what is yet to be seen.

To play and enjoy games, we turn our parents and siblings into good friends. We make friends in our neighborhood, school, church, online, on adventures, and in prison and jails—sometimes even at the dentist's office. When we lose a friend, we make two more, and we move on. By high school, we have good friends and best friends, who make trips to the mall more fun and interesting. Fun actions that instill lifetime memories are better when friends come along. A twosome is good, threesome is awesome, and a group is the best. The exchange of experience, learned skills or imitation of good behavior, the stunts, the enrichment of sexual knowledge, survival skills, emotional support, protection, and many other things in life are some of the benefits of friendship. I am so glad we evolved this way but so sad that friends can turn into enemies.

Friends turn into enemies when life throws something at us that we never fully understand. We learn that things happen for a reason, but they always happen mysteriously, with bad consequences—at least that's how they seem to happen. So yes, wonders of life touch friendships too.

You are not the only one with regrets about having bad friends or the stupidity of good friends. Consider Anthony, whose parents were financially secure. Anthony had a lot friends and best friends. He trusted Manny with some of his secrets and a lot of information about his parents, including where they hid some of their money. Manny had the intention of getting his hands on the property that didn't belong to him. He came to Anthony's house with girls, and as they were having fun with the girls, Manny's friends were robbing Anthony's house of cash and jewelry, all arranged by Manny. Manny's friends weren't so smart, though. They left fingerprints that matched their long criminal records.

As another example, I once went with two friends to a nightclub. Sitting at the bar next to us was a young married couple, and we engaged in friendly bar conversation with them. In no time, we were telling stories and more stories. At one point, the wife asked one of my friends to dance. And then they danced to another song and then another. My friend couldn't leave her alone. They were dancing clean, but the husband asked me if my friend was trying to pick up his wife. I assured the man that my friend was a gentleman. At the same time, I warned my friend about the husband's jealousy, but he didn't want to listen to me. He assured me that he knew what he was doing, and what I needed to do was relax and let him have his fun—except a couple of minutes later, the wife advised us to leave because her husband had called the cops on us.

We hadn't done anything criminal in the club, but we had some unresolved issues with the law, and we didn't want to take any chances. We left in a rush and came across a couple of police cruisers, racing to the club. Had the cops gotten their hands on us, the night would definitely have given us trouble.

When friendships go bad, the damage to your life depends on the kind of action taken and the type of friends in action. Online friends, for example, often cause less pain and disaster than your close friends, unless they steal your identity and credit card information. On the other hand, your best friend, the one with whom you share your darkest secrets, is the one who gives you the knockout blow of betrayal. In most cases, the betrayal of your best friend destroys your life or leaves it in a coma for a long time. It also turns your best friend into your worst enemy. Lucky you, if you are not a victim of cheating.

Snitching and gossip are considered friendship speed bumps. They usually cause a temporary freeze of the friendship, unless some secret, sensitive matters are revealed, and that brings immediate death to friendship. Nothing, however, can compare to the evilness of money among friends. It always causes long-term damage, including the loss of friendship and money. Let's look into how to deal with this troublemaker, money.

To avoid the drama, every time you lend or borrow cash from your friends, make sure a promissory note is received or given. This way, the borrower promises to pay back what he or she borrowed. It is also the guarantee that if the friendship and money can't be saved, the money will be saved in court. The promissory note does seem to signify lack of trust among friends and an uncomfortable feeling among best friends. You see, your friends borrow money from you when things are rough; it's kind of a cry for help. You want to stand as a helpful friend. Asking a friend for a promissory note could kill the purpose of friendship, but "money is evil."

Evil or not, it's your money. If you lend it to somebody, you should get it back. So whenever you lend more than two hundred dollars, you should get a promissory note. And to avoid all the discomfort, make your friend understand your reasons. We all have been ripped off by friends who borrowed and never paid us back. And there you have it—a true common reason.

There are times when you feel confident about getting your money back, because your friend borrowed before and paid you back without problems. That's fine, except that confidence is not assurance. Things can happen and make it impossible for your friend to keep his word without a promissory note. After all, if your friend has the intention of paying you back, he or she wouldn't question the need of a promissory note.

Another aspect that can destroy a friendship is when you have a lot of money, and you lend it to some of your friends. They won't worry about keeping their word to repay, because you are rich. As a matter of fact, their friendship is supported by your money, nothing else. So be aware and take precautions. If you are rich, you should help your buddies in need. But when they borrow from you, you should be paid back. By the way, a witness can be as good as a promissory note, especially if you have more than one.

Fortunately, as we grow older, so does our innocence and understanding of the importance of friends and friends' quality. Hurtful experiences— black eyes, stolen items, stolen boyfriends and girlfriends, lies, and snitching—make us realize that not all friends are who we thought they were. But in fact, betrayal and disastrous experiences involving friends are part of the side effects of friendships. And since we can't live without friends, those experiences should wake up our awareness to bring wisdom in selecting good friends and leave the others at a distance, to minimize those troubles.

From an early age, we receive guidance from our parents and help from friends in selecting friends. Parents keep a close eye on the kinds of kids we want for friends. We may think it's unfair for our parents to stick their noses in the matters of choosing friends. Then, when our friends disappoint us, we turn around and tell our parents, "I guess you were right."

Remember, if your friends are street boys, gang members, pot smokers, or young mothers on welfare, that's what you'll become. If they are honor-roll students, school-musical members, and church-goers, that is what you will become. Know who you are and what you want to be before you make friends. If you have bad characteristics, choose friends with characteristics different from yours. It might be difficult for you in the beginning, but with time, you will absorb the good characteristics of your friends. That's how the game goes in here.

Remember, too, that you are a friend. Never do to others what you don't like done to you. Pack yourself with strong personal qualities and stand as a loyal friend, all the time. Let me warn you, though, that being the best friend you can be doesn't mean you will get the same treatment from all your friends. You will still find some of them disrespecting your feelings and philosophical principles, but this is not about what your friends are to you. This is about what you are to your friends.

When you bring the characteristics of a good friend into your life, you will benefit, because you will become a better person. You will become more likable and easily fit in any social arena. Like attracts like, and birds of a feather flock together.

How do you turn bad experiences into good ones? Whenever you're a victim of a bad experience with a friend, never go for the common hateful behavior of a vengeful response carried out with weapons. Use the methods of sweet revenge. For example, if your friends snitch and bad-mouth you, drop them and get better friends. If your best friend sleeps with your lover, replace them with the best around, put yourself on higher ground, and let jealousy and regrets take care of your traitors. If a friend makes you lose your job, get another one that he or she can only dream of. Whatever the case, find the appropriate sweet revenge, and work at it until you achieve it. That's how you turn bad experiences into loving memories. That's how you put yourself ahead of the game. That's how you tell your bad friends, "Look at me now!" And don't be afraid to show the world your new friends.

From whatever way friendship came to us, it soon became part of our basic needs—the main ingredient of human civilization and survival, a balance of humanity. You are meant to live with friends from the beginning to the end; you are human. For if you live a friendless life, you are not living. You could do well without friends, especially when you are self-sufficient, but in reality, you would live a sad life. Do you want to stay ahead of the game? Good! Friends will help you do that.

8

Race and Discrimination

I WAS TAUGHT IN SCHOOL that life began in Africa. By comparing blood proteins and the DNA of the African great apes with those of humans, studies have concluded that human beings (hominids) split off from the great apes about eight million years ago. And if it's true, then all of us are Negroes from Africa. And that being true puts us in the path of understanding that we, all of us, are the breakdown of the first generation—black.

From the first generation, assumed to be millions of years old, up to us, many transformations—mutations, revolutions, and evolution—happened, and I think they continue to happen, even when we don't notice. At times, these transformations happen internally; other times they are due to our interaction with the ecosystem; and other times they are a result of the combination of both. Whatever the case, it brings brain development and physical changes for adaptation to the new world.

About two million years ago, things began to spice up. The first of our ancestors moved out of Africa, either because the habitat became unbearable or because the genes of curiosity pushed them to discover the mystery beyond the horizon, and they decided to stay at one of the paradises they found, and their descendents migrated to the entire globe.

They also exposed themselves to a new ecosystem and obviously had to adjust to the new environment and lifestyle, and probably a new culture, tradition, and sexual interaction during the exodus. This reality, with time, could turn a black man to a less black man and could allow women to deliver babies not quite black. You never know what can come out of chaos, especially when chaos lingers for millions of years. And so there you have it: a real white descendent from a real black ancestor, whose family tree went through all kinds of chaos for millions of years. Or it could be that God created us in different ways, shapes, forms, and colors, and then threw us into the wild, and then sat down, relaxed, and probably sipped a good wine, while watching us develop into the devils we became.

There are tons of probabilities about our origin, development, and identity that could have escaped the science of human evolution. There is so much that we know that we don't know! But we know that regardless of whether we are black, white, green, red, yellow, or whatever, there is always a one-of-a-kind in all tribes—the big thinkers, such as Albert Einstein, Pablo Picasso, Isaac Newton, Leonardo da Vinci, Plato, Aristotle, Sigmund Freud, and many others. These are the ones who came up with impressive ways of improving our lives. The rest of us will respect and follow their ideas. This reality can be the first factor in class division. And unfortunately, everything that's born or created usually grows and multiplies.

In this perspective, I don't know if whites got the supremacy from the very beginning or if blacks got it first and then lost it to whites, but it seems that whites moved ahead of all races and fought hard to protect the throne. When the class difference reached the point of slavery, blacks lost all chance of turning around, because the two had grown too far apart. Blacks, in a sense, lost human status.

In other places where blacks were still considered human, the lack of opportunity to get an education pushed them even farther behind. And whites did an excellent job of preventing others from getting the means to advance. Apparently, they led others to believe that blacks couldn't advance in life because they were an inferior race, incapable of learning anything. Blacks, however, didn't accept it, believing that God created all men as equals and that there should not be white supremacy, black inferiority, or any social division based entirely on race. And in the process of one proving the other wrong, society went through hell because of racism.

If you are a nonwhite and believe in white supremacy, your expectations are low. You may have no goals in life or zero drive to do anything about your dreams. You accept what is given to you by whites, as you understand that whites are in full charge of your destiny. Some still believe this myth and are submissive to whites.

Those who did not believe this myth but considered whites an impossible obstacle on the road to success for nonwhites created the hate toward whites. Then the third group, who didn't believe that racism stood in the way of individuals' success, made sacrifices and proved the myth wrong by becoming well-educated, rich, famous, and powerful blacks: Bill Cosby, Sidney Poitier, Morgan Freeman, Samuel L. Jackson, Denzel Washington, Arsenio Hall, Danny Glover, Louis Gossett Jr., Spike Lee, Eddie Murphy, Will Smith, Martin Lawrence, Laurence Fishburne, Wesley Snipes, Forest Whitaker, Whoopi Goldberg, Halle Berry, Queen Latifah, Nat King Cole, Jimi Hendrix, Ray Charles, Michael Jackson, Stevie Wonder, Bob Marley, John Lee Hooker, Calvin Cordozar Broadus Jr. (Snoop Dog), Tupac Shakur, Christopher George (Biggie), Kanye West, James Todd Smith (LL Cool J), Christopher Brian Bridges (Ludacris), Dwayne Michael Carter Jr. (Lil Wayne), Shawn Corey Carter (Jay-Z), Aretha Franklin, Tina Turner, Janet Jackson, Whitney Houston, Vanessa Williams, Missy Elliott, Shaquille O'Neal, Magic Johnson, Charles Barkley, Julius Erving, Wilt Chamberlain, Lynette Woodard, Michael Jordan, Walter Payton, Jim Brown, Leroy "Satchel" Paige, Jackie Robinson, Hank Aaron, Kareem Abdul-Jabbar, Arthur Ashe, Serena Williams, Venus Williams, Althea Gibson, Sugar Ray Leonard, Sugar Ray Robinson, Muhammad Ali, Joe Frasier, George Foreman, Mike Tyson, Evander Holyfield, Rubin "Hurricane" Carter, Reggie Jackson, Bo Jackson, Jackie Joyner-Kersee, Carl Lewis, Tiger Woods, Malcolm X, Martin Luther King Jr., Rosa Parks, Nelson Mandela, and Barack Obama—just to mention a few among many others on the long list of successful black people who realized that hard work, determination, and serious commitment are some of the important requirements for success in life.

When they encountered racism in their path, they didn't freeze, because they knew that racism is part of social composition that will stick around for as long as we do, despite the efforts of human rights movements to eliminate it. These successful black people stayed focused on the final prize, not on the pain and anguish to get there. Every time they fell, they got up twice as strong and stayed the course, proving wrong those who said they couldn't do it.

For those of you who were born with nothing at all, stop complaining, drop your freaking hoodies, cut the braids, tie your shoes, fasten your belt, and go to college and university to earn your success. It doesn't matter who you are or where you are. "If you can think it, you can do it." And if you are in the United States of America—the land of the free and the home of the brave—there's no excuse for you not to be what you want to be. Get on the right track, and do whatever you must do for yourself and your country. Destiny makes things happen with who you are and what you have, not what you wish you had. If you keep waiting for the perfect wave of destiny to wash over you, you may go home with dry feet.

Supremacy

Maybe whites had a head start. Maybe whites were smarter. Maybe whites were more powerful. Maybe whites dominated all other colors. It seems that many whites believed that and took it to heart. They showed it by hatred and racism, which actually destroyed them. But in reality, we are all one part of a big whole, and we will never fully understand it if we lack the true knowledge of the origin of it. What's clear is that we can't deny brotherhood. Every time we cut or get cut, we drop blood of the same color. Every time we go to the bathroom, we discharge waste of the same kind. And finally, from dust we came and to the dust we shall return.

If you carry anger and hatred toward any race or color, I desperately hope that one day you will wake up and smell the roses. Maybe it's true that your ancestors were victims of physical torture and the indignity of sexual assaults as slaves, and your ancestors were hanged by the Ku Klux Klan. Maybe it's true that the government makes it look like the only business you can run is the one on the street corners, the only ability you have is taking what is not yours, and the only paradise you can have is the one protected by guards and barbwire. Maybe rehab is phony and youth programs are just a waste of time and taxpayer money. Maybe the government is aiming to keep you addicted for life and keep ghetto youth in the projects, shooting and stabbing each other. Maybe police brutality is for blacks and other minorities, and protection is for the white neighborhoods only.

Maybe that's all true, but you don't have to buy what the government or anybody is selling to you, especially if it pushes you deeper into your troubles. You also don't have to blame the government, your parents, or your in-laws for inflicting misery, pain, and suffering in your life for raising you in the wrong places. Stop finding excuses for not getting out of the mud, and understand the world and humanity. Wishing that the world was fair or hoping that you could wake up tomorrow sipping gold and spitting out silver in a one-color world is a comedy. The joke will be on you. Packing guns and bullets to shoot your enemies and killing innocent children to relieve your anger or to prove a point will not change a thing either. Actually, it will change things for the worst—you first. Even if you succeed in carrying out your savage plan, as with the massacre in Oslo, Norway, in July 2011, you haven't moved an inch toward human greatness. You are letting the evil within be in charge of your destiny.

Whatever way racism came to us, it has walked with us from the very beginning. It has destroyed lives, and it continues destroying lives in all forms and shapes. It still leaves society bullied by sucker punches, but we have been taking turns too. It's like we started out as single color— something I truly believe—and now we are walking toward the beginning of the circle to be a one-color society, one hugely large nation under one president, under one God—again. You can enjoy the best life has to offer and create something special of yourself, or you can form your squad and go on a journey of supremacy. The choice is yours. You can continue to live your miserable life of ignorance and racism with hatred to other colors, which will drive you to zero, or you can wake up and help yourself and those around you to become heroes. Racism will only slow you down or stop you from advancing in life.

Some things we can change; other things we must accept—never forget that.

Discrimination

A dictionary definition of discrimination is the "treatment or consideration of, or making a distinction in favor of or against, a person or thing based on the group, class, or category to which that person or thing belongs rather than on individual merit." To that, I would add race. I find it almost impossible to be racist without using discrimination. We could confuse things, however, by thinking that only racism discriminates.

Discrimination happens among people of the same race, color, or type. It is driven by emotions, which makes it impossible to control it. It exists in us, and I don't think it will ever go away. In large families, mothers and fathers naturally love one child more than another. It could be some specific physical difference or personality that happens to grab the heart of the mother or father. The same thing happens between siblings, friends, coworkers, or neighbors. Your heart chooses for you, and it becomes almost impossible to fight it. You shouldn't. There's no need for it. But when your discrimination becomes hurtful, especially to others, you should do something about it. At that point, you must understand that you do not have to hate those you don't like. Not everybody likes you either, but you wouldn't like to be hurt by them. There are times when those we dislike in the beginning will turn into our friends after we interact with them. I am not suggesting that we force ourselves to be friends, but if we understand discrimination and keep it from causing harm to us and others, we can share and enjoy this world more.

We all want to live in a perfect world. That probably isn't possible—if a perfect world existed, we would make it imperfect. We must understand, however, that we need to respect each other and learn to share with love and peace and by honoring the brotherhood we carry inside.

9

Communication

ANOTHER TRAIT THAT DISTINGUISHES US from other animals is the ability to communicate verbally. It is a great tool to help us succeed on the journey of life. Unfortunately, most of us are poorly equipped in the world of communication. Many factors, such as education, culture, philosophy, and political regime are to blame for this. We might grow up in a family that doesn't allow us to express our feelings, thoughts, and emotions freely. It might be more like a military style of life, where we aren't allowed to ask questions or give an opinion. This type of oppression inhibits children's ability to develop the power of communication. When the time comes that communication is necessary in the outside world, they are handicapped.

For example, in committed relationships, the fuel to keep peace and understanding flowing and the flames of love glowing is not there. The communication oppression from childhood shows up in the form of dominance in arguments, as a way to compensate for the loss of freedom of speech during childhood. The normal communication processes is no longer a peaceful way of conveying your ideas to others and listening to their responses. It becomes all about "You listen to me. I don't have to listen to you." We focus on what we plan to say next instead of listening to what has been said to us.

But in general, miscommunication is dominant in almost all dysfunctional relationships. Communication almost always ends up in an ugly argument. So the couples avoid confrontation by holding thoughts until they can't stand it anymore, and then they explode. Also, the weaker the power of communication—learned from education, life experiences, and so on—the greater the consequences of miscommunication.

Whether inside or outside our homes, we get messed up. And the reason is simple: we can talk, but we can't communicate well. To communicate well, we have to learn the skills and improve on them. Some people say that Mitt Romney lost the presidential race, in part, because Republicans had no message, and they had the worst communicator to deliver it.

The power of communication is the switch of the chain reaction. If you are a good communicator, you will have a good job in public relations, create friends with ease, and get better jobs. You will be likable, and your relationships will be loving, because your lover won't be afraid to speak his or her mind. Talking to you is never a confrontation. What can you do to help achieve this goal?

- Read (everything). It enriches your vocabulary, keeps you updated with the world, and unshackles your brain to exercise the thinking process.
- Write (about anything). It helps you to take your thoughts out of your head and put them on paper.
- Become a politician. Disagree intellectually just to exercise your ability to bring across your points of view.
- Take communication courses. This one is the best foundation for improving your communication skills.

When you must stay silent because your education level didn't allow you to improve your communication skills, you become the victim of circumstance. There's probably not much you can do. For the rest of us, there's no excuse. Communication must be a priority. Maybe everything can't be good in life, but it is your duty to fight for survival. We are all in this together. You may have the power to win the battle, and now you need the communication skills to win the war. The conflict is not over until you win both the battle and the war.

The biggest problem in relationships is lack of communication.

One of the best ingredients in communication is listening.

10

Confidence

To PLAY A GOOD GAME and win big, you need to consider a few things: the hand you have, knowledge of the game, your level of competition, and confidence. In the game of life, you have to take a few more things into consideration, but the points mentioned above also stand.

We know that fear is born within us, and it will never go away. Fear is part of who we are. It evolves with us for obvious safety reasons, but we also know that there is a remedy for fear: experience. Don't make the mistake of believing that fear goes away forever. What you are able to do, however, is keep your fear under control and not let it paralyze you.

When I was a high school freshman, I fell in love with every beautiful girl, but fear prevented me from getting even one single love. The reality of getting a girl was a bit different then; there wasn't such a thing as asking for a phone number. You would have to win over a girl through long and seductive conversation. Even when you were blessed with the first date, you didn't know what was to come.

In my sophomore year, I found myself madly in love with a beautiful, tall white girl with long dark hair. Slender like an acoustic guitar, with firm breasts and sexy long legs, she just ate my heart out. She didn't have the most beautiful face in the high school, but she had a distinctive seductive move that covered any little flaws—if there were any. I couldn't have seen any, because passion blinded me to anything that could seem imperfect in her.

She knew that she was beautiful, influential, and powerful. She didn't have many friends, but she wasn't antisocial either. Her innocence translated into simplicity, and she knew how to use her gifts. Her father was an airline pilot. Flying was a luxury career, granted to the best of the best with special connections. For that, she would be the first one to have the most beautiful watches and all the fancy electronic toys. She never needed to do much to radiate her beauty and social status. Everybody talked about her—Maria John.

Every chance I had, I got closer to her and made sure she realized that I was looking, impressed, and in love. I thought of so many things to say but had a horrendous fear of expressing my feelings to women. It seemed there were millions of instances in which I got very close to her, and I rehearsed what I wanted to say millions of times, but I never gathered enough courage.

One Tuesday, after class, I was prayed not to lose the opportunity. I saw her exit the school through the main door and wait for her father to pick her up. Most students had already left. She was almost alone, and that was the perfect opportunity. So I approached her and said, "Maria John, I need to speak to you, but this is not a good time. Could you come to Esplanade at six o'clock, and we can talk?" (Esplanade was a small outdoor restaurant in the town's main square.) I don't remember how fast I said those words to her in my shaking voice, but I know for sure that my heart would have won the Boston marathon. I can't believe I didn't collapse. I couldn't believe her response either—she agreed to meet.

I walked home faster than ever, happier than I'd ever been. I couldn't wait, so I decided to go much earlier and wait for her. As the time to meet her approached, my heart began to race. More than once, fear almost made me get up and go home, but I couldn't lose that opportunity. I was about to enter paradise. This is what had been torturing me. I had to wait for her and talk to her. I'd taken the biggest step. I had ventured way beyond the courage of so many of my schoolmates, who were going through the same torture but didn't dare to ask her out.

Each second closer to six o'clock, I looked anxiously to see if she was coming. She didn't. There was no sign of her. At times, that was fine with me; at other times, I felt she was playing with me.

At 6:20, there was still no sign of her. Definitely convinced that she'd played me, I left Esplanade and walked to the high school. I had seen her hanging around after school on the high school grounds, so there was a chance she was there. I walked around the grounds but couldn't find her.

Disappointed, with a sharp arrow stuck in my heart, I decided to go for a walk in town. At about halfway between the high school and Esplanade, I saw what appeared to be an angel walking toward me from the opposite direction. It didn't take me long to realize that it was Maria John. This time, she was dressed to kill.

Apparently, I wasn't thinking straight. I didn't know what to do. I didn't know how I would start the conversation. I was lost, and we were approaching each other fast. When we reached each other, I said hello; she responded with hello. Like strangers, however, I continued walking south; she did the same toward the north. And right there, it was the end of us—something didn't begin, thanks to fear.

The relationship between fear and confidence is simple: the greater the fear, the lesser the confidence. Once you move beyond fear, however, experience is what will bring confidence. And once you have enough confidence, you will sit at the table to play the game of life. You will not be afraid of any game. Whatever hand you are dealt, you will manage to do well or beat your opponents. Now you won't have to go to the game early to find a seat. There will be plenty of empty seats, because you will play with the big boys. Better yet, at this level of the game, you will be a winner, even when you lose. Prioritize your experiences in your life to bring a broad range of confidence to you.

The first time we asked a girl out, it seemed like we were walking in the tunnel of frightening events. But as we continued to ask more people out, the fear diminished, to the point that it became a simple thing. In our first job interview, we performed poorly and likely did not get the job.

On subsequent interviews, though, our performance did not stop us from getting the job, because we had developed confidence in job interviews. Professional speakers go through hell in their first public event—they can't wait for the torture to end—but as they keep performing, each next appearance is less frightening.

Confidence rocks, and experience is what gives you confidence. It empowers you to face any game, and it makes you stay focused on scoring big, without worrying about winning, because you know that you can't lose.

Your attitude toward life can be a boost to or a drag on your success. If you wash your brain with a negative attitude, you will become a loser. Fill your head with a positive attitude in all circumstances. Don't complain about your car breaking down on your way to a job interview and your not having the money to fix it. Of course, it's unfortunate if your son breaks his arm while riding on his skateboard, and you have no health insurance. But understand that when such things happen, it's part of what happens to everybody in different ways. These are the low cards we all get now and then. It doesn't mean that we should slam those cards on the table and walk away from the game. We stay, using our skills, competitiveness, and attitude to win the game. Even when we are touched by bad experiences, there's a good side to it—they become the ingredients that build our confidence. Do not let the madness of such incidents take away your power to move on with confidence. Snap out of it, cool off, and use your head to think. After all, you will get your car fixed, and your son will heal. A better way to deal with bad experiences is to use the confidence you built through other experiences, good and bad.

Fear, action, and confidence go together. Confidence reduces fear, and action brings confidence. That means you must do something different all the time. Some experts say that you should face your fears; others say the opposite. I personally suggest that you pick something in the middle and that you experiment to increase your confidence. For example, if you are terrified of being lost when you go out of town, pick a Saturday or Sunday morning to cruise, alone or with company. Make sure your GPS is working, but don't use it. Try to intentionally get lost, and then find your way home using your own sense and by asking people for directions. If you can't find your way back, then use the GPS. This is just one example of things you can do to help overcome fear and increase your confidence.

Competitiveness and Attitude

Competitiveness is a plus in the game of life. It gives you a boost to come up with strategies to win. It gives you the edge to make yourself the most valuable player when everybody is struggling to stay in the game. It will bring out the urge to go home as a winner every day, no matter how tough the game was. Competitiveness is also born within us. Some of us have more competitiveness than others, and sometimes that can be bad for the game of life. Then it's our responsibility to make sure we take only what is good from competitiveness. Although a strong competitiveness gives you an edge, it can also be harmful—it can drive you to actions that can kill, create enemies, or bring a high level of stress and frustration.

My son William, at age seven, was bike racing with his friends but not winning all the races. He asked his uncle to let him use his adult bike, even though William could barely pedal it! When his uncle asked him why, William said that with the adult bike, he would pass everybody. (Son, that was smart thinking, but it could have injured you!) The crazy spirit of competitiveness should be toned down to avoid ill effects.

My youngest son, Christopher, made amazing progress in martial arts because he had a highly competitive spirit. In no time, he became one of the best students, easily surpassing his schoolmates. When he got his brown belt, a mother of another student told me, "Wow, Christopher is flying!" Indeed!

Shortly after Chris got his junior black belt, Hamid Lahrizi, the best martial arts instructor in the area and the owner of Hamid's Academy, the best school in the area, took his teaching to a new level by adding acrobatics to the American mixed martial arts style. He came up with this competition between the best students for a beautiful, unique uniform. The final challenge came down to my son and Romani, a younger student who was coming up fast to become the best of the best. Romani won the competition. My son accepted the loss, but he was angry.

When we got home, he threw himself on the bed, covered his head, and talked to nobody. I felt his pain, but I knew there wasn't anything I could do to ease his pain, so I left him alone.

The next day when he returned from school in a better mood, he told me that he was "over it." He understood that he couldn't have everything; he couldn't win all the time. His highly competitive spirit was not as dangerous as his brother William's but still crazy.

On the other hand, low competitiveness puts you in the disadvantage chair—the chair of an easy game with cheap or no prizes. You are automatically behind the real game. You play the easy games of welfare and sit at other entitlement tables, which some call the table of destitute losers. Others call it the table of suckers. I call it the table of the less fortunate. But it doesn't matter what you call it; that table is not the table of the best game in life, and you should avoid it at all costs. One of the ways you can get away from that table and move to a better one is by increasing your competitiveness. Look at your friends and neighbors who are doing better than you are and promise yourself you will be where they are—or ahead of them—whatever it takes.

If that seems like too much or impossible for you to do, you can find ways to increase your spirit of competitiveness. It will help you gain confidence and move you to higher ground.

Your attitude can be a drastic setback or a great push. If you have a negative attitude toward life, you have less of a chance of success, because your determination to fight for what you want in life is zero. You will wait for people to give it to you instead of creating your own dreams and making plans to make them come true.

A negative attitude is your worst enemy, but a positive attitude is your best friend. The positive, active attitude takes you a long way along the path of boosting your confidence, which in turn helps you stay ahead of the game.

11

Employment

AGES AGO, PARENTS PUSHED THEIR kids to be lawyers, doctors, and engineers, or at least to get a college degree so they would be set for life. Small certifications gave good jobs; big certifications gave six-figure incomes. Big certifications came with a guide to Wall Street as one of the options to score big. When the whole world is financially stable, employment is abundant and job security is firm. Almost all sectors of employment have job positions available. There could be more jobs available than people to fill the positions, and the chance of getting the job you like and that pays well is greater.

Unfortunately, nothing stays the same. It's only a matter of time before nature strikes again with disaster after disaster, or a financial scheme reaches scandal stage and spins the wheels of chaos. In the case of natural strikes, there's nothing to do other than clean up the mess, pick up the pieces, and rebuild again.

Financial scandal is a completely different story. It also strikes harder. When the roots of the scheme are detected, those found responsible are sent to or go on trial. Large businesses begin layoffs; small businesses do the same. Government panics. The country where the scheme was born will roll up its sleeves and face the consequences.

We woke up in economic turbulence, followed by an economic earthquake, followed by an economic tsunami, all triggered by the housing bubble—presumably thanks to Wall Street. As we gathered strength to clean up the mess, and it started to look clean, some Eastern sandstorms or Western dust storms came to mess up the area again. We know the East is there, but we don't know which way West is. The reverse blow from globalization is not helping either. Highly educated, poorly educated, and uneducated are struggling in different boats but in the same water.

Also, as the gap between rich and poor widens, the angry 99 percent spread their complaints worldwide, and the economic bounce brings frustration with its uncertainty. Monthly job creations don't cover the number of lost jobs, and manufacturers and corporations go to China and India because, among other business conveniences, labor is cheaper and regulations are not as tight.

The world economy has always had its ups and downs. All world wars, besides the horrifying bloodshed and massive loss of innocent lives, caused economic chaos worldwide. We are not facing another world war in the sense of the two previous world wars, but we certainly are facing as bad or worse an economic consequence of world wars of the past. We don't seem to find ways to get out of this bad world economy fast enough to give us the chance to enjoy a life from good employment, especially the one we earned through higher education.

Catching Up to Technology

In the 1980s, there was the computer age, and technology spread out fast. The rest of the world saw the power and prosperity of big nations, thanks to computer science and manufacturing, so it wanted to step up to the plate by incorporating the amazingly impressive machines performing tasks faster and more efficiently than human beings.

People looking for a new career path should look no farther: the computer field is the best, it is here, and it is here to stay. I took the first available computer training in Cape Verde Islands in 1988. Many friends pointed to computers as the promising career path for generations to come.

Manufacturers, in an attempt to reach new customers and increase sales, have made computer software easy to use, taking the people with a low level of education into the computer world by offering home computers at a price that almost anybody can afford and making them simple to operate. This economic strategy has attracted people from all corners of life into the world of computers. Basic computer skills, once an advantage on résumés, became commonplace. Now, anyone who does not know how to perform the basic tasks on a computer is ridiculed, as kids as young as two years old can operate a computer. Lacking basic computer skills puts you out of the job market in almost all fields of employment; proficiency gives you a small edge, but you must have many other qualifications to land yourself a good job in the computer field. One way to avoid missing the best jobs is by staying current with technological developments and by upgrading your skills. But the fight doesn't stop here, because in general, as getting an education becomes easier, more qualified people will be on the job market.

This reality tells you that when you're looking for a job, you will find a heavy load of people searching for the same thing as you are, often with qualifications better than yours.

Continuation of Education

The harsh blow comes after high school graduation. You might think, "After twelve years of torturing my head with things that don't make sense and that I know I will never use in my entire life, I am not going back to school!" Actually, it's to your advantage to continue learning.

You see, the knowledge you accumulate during high school is not enough to carry you throughout your career. If you cut yourself off from continuing education, when you are faced with the urgency of upgrading your skills, you will regret your decision to stay away from school. It will be more difficult to wake up your brain after many years of sleepiness. High school graduation is just a license to place one foot into the house of knowledge. The real deal starts right here and right now. All you've learned during the first twelve school years is only the supporting blocks in the building of your wisdom and true education.

After the graduation celebration, the real job of making your dreams come true begins. And if you say good-bye to school after that graduation day, chances are that when your class meets for a reunion, all you'll have to show is mountains of failures.

Consider it mandatory to stay in touch with education until the day you die. Now, staying in touch doesn't mean you never leave the classroom. Some of the alternatives are online courses, home studies, seminars, or even reading good books. And this means that there's no excuse for you not to continue your education—it's a must.

Education and Job Mismatch

Interpreting greed as a good thing, after misunderstanding the movie *Wall Street*, sent graduates of business schools straight to Wall Street, aiming to get rich fast. The recipe for success in *Wall Street* appeared to be learning how to be corrupt. Why go to school to become a doctor or a lawyer, only to face a lifetime of school debt, fights with insurance, lawsuits, and risk of losing your license due to errors and mistakes?

Since the 1960s, many countries have become independent by pursuing wealth and international recognition. Also, the population growth allows more geniuses to walk among us. Media propaganda and reality TV featuring rich people's lives awaken the desire in the rest of us to be one of them. And for better or for worse, the world truly has become one large, crazy, greedy family. And so, new grads, you might have the potential tools to help you succeed in your after-graduation journey, but you have a battle ahead of you. There will be few available positions in your area of expertise. Minimum-wage jobs and landscaping are pretty much what you can rely on for cash. But even with a minimum-wage job, you have to stand up to the competition. Actually, manual labor is where the competition is the most ferocious, because this type of work doesn't require special skills— anybody can do it. You are competing with a heavy flow of unskilled immigrants, high school dropouts, and laid-off employees looking for anything to make a weekly check. It is a chronic employment illness from top to bottom. Health care is the only branch with open spots, but that's not for you right now, and it has its backlash—among other things, it's demanding and the schedule is very unforgiving.

Your only hope is that the economy doesn't take forever to get back on its feet, because that could put you in a position to take additional courses to upgrade your skills so you can compete. Just being a couple of years out of touch could make you rusty and put you out of the job market.

The Power of Higher Education

Having to face this reality after you have graduated can give you a few migraines and make you start wondering if it was worth spending so much money to earn yourself a higher education, which left you with tens of thousands of dollars in school loans and without a job. Meanwhile, your buddy who dropped out of high school years ago is now a small-business owner, probably struggling but on his feet. And how about those who dropped out of school on Wednesday and went on with their ideas to become billionaires by Sunday? You may want to shoot yourself, as your higher education gives you headaches and takes you nowhere.

But don't be fooled. Never forget that education occupies no space, and it is the only treasure you take to the grave. Higher education now serves you as a powerful tool to help you understand where we all fit and where we are heading, as well as see the options that are left for us and how to cope with stress and disappointment.

In this messed-up world with a bad economy, your higher education will help you understand that you are blessed to have a job and not to count on paradise at your workplace. Your higher education helps you understand the reality of your situation and how to handle it, as well as the options you have. Follow rules, regulations, and procedures and be as friendly as you can, even if that is not who you are. No matter how much you dread going to work, keep your thoughts to yourself. Make positive comments about the workplace, and make your coworkers understand that the workplace is not as bad as it seems—even if it is. Teach yourself never to make negative comments about the management and bosses, because whatever you say today will get to their ears tomorrow. You may have heard that in the workplace, the walls have ears. It is true. That's one way people know about your secret bitching and snitching. Remember that people don't know how to keep secrets. And you know better than to bad-mouth your company on Facebook, because you know they are watching and listening.

Your higher education helps you understand your coworkers. Keep those with a short temper at a distance, and keep those with common sense close to you. Take orders from your superiors in the company, even if it's unfair, because then you'll have a good working relationship. It would be foolish to abandon a job because of rules, regulations, and procedures that you consider stupid or unfair. You simply need to adjust to what you have, instead of moving to another workplace. You will find the same or worse reality at a new workplace, and it could take you months of unemployment before you get another job.

Résumé

Anytime you need a good résumé, all you need to do is go online and get all the information you need to create one. What will kill you with regard to your résumé is your own stupidity. By that I mean lying about your qualifications on your résumé. Create a résumé that is true to you, your skills, and your personality, and then prepare to wrap it up nicely with a well-prepared interview.

Choosing Your Workplace

One of the main steps now is to be realistic about your potential, skills, and abilities. Next is to pick a career path that fits the description of your personality, matches your desires, and has economic potential. From this point on, reaching any accomplishment ahead requires more time than you have. Don't spend money and years of studies at a college or university to get just shy of graduation and realize that you made a big mistake; that you should have chosen a different school or career path.

Many businesses and organizations can help you choose a career path. Gather all the information possible before starting the new, long journey. Try to decide what you want to be, years before you graduate high school. Students who do that have a greater chance of success, as they waste no time waiting for inspiration to decide a career path for them. And once you have that out of the way, you have already passed the hardest point— making a firm decision about what you want to be for the rest of your life. You may choose to follow the family tradition, or you may decide to go your own way and choose a career that's outside the family tradition.

In a good economy, choosing a workplace is like eating cake—you take one piece here and one piece there, until your taste buds tell you which cake is best. In a bad economy, there are only a few pieces to choose from, flavors are reduced, and more people stand in line to grab a piece. You might be lucky to make it to a table but then find out that the cake is all gone. Still, you might not dare to wait for the second round because it could take forever. So you take what is there, and you tell your taste buds to stop complaining and enjoy what they have.

Choosing a workplace in a bad economy is no fun, but here are some of the things you should take into consideration to help you prepare:

- *Qualifications.* A diploma and certification from well-known schools, places of previous employment, and written references are part of your qualifications to boost your confidence.
- *Competition.* No matter which skills and qualifications you have, don't assume that you are the one because you have the elite package. Others with equal or better packages are heading to the same place you are. But that doesn't mean you should back down. Gear yourself for the fight and sharpen your weaponry, keeping in mind that your opponents are doing the same. That should help you accept second or third place.
- *Opportunities and threats.* Go online and search the company where you are interested in working. Just be aware that information

online is not necessarily 100 percent correct. Also, talk with employees. The amount of information you will need depends on how interested you are in working there. Do your homework and compare what you are told in the interview with information you gathered yourself. You need to know about the place you are choosing to work, so you can avoid investing years there, only to realize later that you need to go somewhere else. Also, don't think that competition is your only threat. You need to know the future of the workplace.

- *Your potential.* Fancy diplomas and certificates are the strongest tools for getting a job of your dreams, but you must prepare yourself for the fact that other things could stop you from delivering what is expected of you. Always look for other things that can increase your potential in the employment world.

- *Your personality.* Make sure you know who you are before you devote all your energy to a certain workplace. If you are stubborn, selfish, and rude, don't choose a workplace where flexibility, cooperation, and good manners are mandatory.

- *Your dreams.* This one is the one that you should respect the most. Placing yourself in a workplace just to earn a living is a slow, suicidal process that will bring the deadly blow years later, when you look back and realize you made a mistake. The best way to respect your dreams is by moving at full force toward what your dreams are. Sure, circumstances may cause you to take something else as a matter of survival, but the full attention should still go to your dreams, to what you love. Always be on the lookout for ways to embrace your dreams. In fact, there are times when you should ignore small opportunities that will create speed bumps on the road toward your dreams.

- *Stay ahead of the game.* It's your responsibility to understand what you need to do to stay ahead of the game.

Protect What You Have

When you find a workplace of your dreams and are lucky enough to get the job, don't assume that you are set. Then it will be time to fight to make it last. You must use your skills and your head to deliver what you promised and protect what you have—a job, a career. You must stay on your toes to make sure that you have all the bases covered. Stay current, keep your eyes open and your ears alert, and be prepared for nasty surprises. If you are truly passionate about your job or career, broaden your knowledge with regard to what you should do to stay employed. There are numerous books and other support for you.

12

Technology

When I turned seventeen, I fell into the hot wave of the philosophical arena cast by many of my friends who were older and more educated than I was. I remember Paulo, Sergio, Jose Maria, Vladimir (Val), and Olavo engaging in endless arguments, whipped left and right by philosophy, science, math, biology—you name it. What a wonderful circle of knowledge and intellect that was! I was in ninth grade, unable to participate actively but capable of making some careful remarks. And little by little, I became brave enough to engage. Every time we engaged in philosophical debate— that's how we referred to it—the argument would become endless, not only due to the invincible attitude of teenagers, but also because we named ourselves as philosophers who must win the argument at all costs.

A one-on-one argument was always endless. We would put the argument on hold until the next day or until we regrouped, giving others a chance to choose sides and continue the argument with reinforcements. So many times, the main subject was forgotten because we drifted so far from it and sneaked in other subjects to avoid defeat. By the time we reached agreement, we no longer remembered the starting subject. For example, we would start the argument about human powers, bounce to the beauty and complexity of the sea, and then to the ambiguity of religion and doubts about God's existence, and then to cultural differences, and end up closing the argument with the inexistence of the existence of ghosts. When we reached agreement, some of us would hit the "but" key to bring the argument back to life.

We were truly committed to bringing in a point of view from all perspectives! I used to hate it when my team just had convinced the other team, and then I'd hear someone say, "But …" I guess this huge desire to impress and fight to win is strongest in teenagers.

One particular day, Sergio and I were watching a man dig the foundation for a small house in a poor neighborhood. It was about five o'clock. Not far from him was a yellow excavator with the word Caterpillar written in big, bold black letters on the side and back of it. It was parked and unattended, done for the day. It was there to continue government work the next day.

That scenario ignited a philosophical argument. The subject was "technology and education"—how important each one was and their relationship to each other. Sergio leaned toward the benefit to the world when everybody is educated. I disagreed, and the fire began to grow:

"Not everybody can be educated. You know that is impossible. Who will do agriculture, the labors related to it, construction, fishing, and all that?" I asked.

"Machines will be invented to do that," Sergio responded.

"That's not possible."

"Why not?"

"I don't know. I just know that's not possible."

"Nothing is impossible, man!" Sergio argued. "How many men would it take to finish the excavation that Caterpillar is doing?"

"I don't know, and that doesn't matter because I know that not everybody can be educated."

"Why?"

"I told you why!"

His point of view was that even when everybody is highly educated, the hard labor would keep its place. Hard labor would be done with the help of easy-to-use tools. Higher technology would create modern equipment and machinery to make any job more efficient and safer. Basically, it was "work smarter, not harder." He was seeing the world of technology far ahead, except he was so far behind! The machinery we were thinking of was created already, and it was doing a great job in rich countries.

In thinking about what we have become throughout the long journey of humanization, we should pay respect to whatever reasons made us leave the African caves. Vegetarians, carnivores, or whatever, we had to be in the open wild, searching for or collecting food. We were not the only animals in the wild, but we didn't care much about the smaller ones that we could subdue and kill. We had fear of all the others that posed threats and became our competitors.

I don't quite remember what I learned in social studies class about ancient technological development, but I think that need made us create tools, primarily to protect ourselves from invaders and intruders. Then, we kept upgrading our protective and hunting weaponry and skills—from rock throwing to slingshots, to bow and arrow, to spears, to knives, to swords, to shotguns, and so on. Later on, we revolutionized the means of transportation, from walking to animal rides, to caravan, bicycle, motorcycle, canoe, boat, ship, car, train, plane, rocket, and space shuttle.

We progressed from homing pigeons to telegraphs, telephones, Morse code, portable radios or transmitters, beepers for security service, radios, record players, turntables and phonographs, Walkmans, iPods, computers, laptops, and iPhones.

In medicine, we have come all the way from healing simple wounds, aches, and pains to stopping death and regaining life from short death, thanks to human skills and technological advancements, with God's blessing. Let's take our hats off to those fine inventors who keep bringing technological advancement to our lives.

The Ups and Downs

Any time geniuses come up with something fantastic, the devil pours his evil on it (just to spice things up a little bit)—the military, terrorists, cheaters, and others find ways to modify the application of the new toy for their own good. In addition, technologies designed to make our lives easier and interesting have their side effects. For example, innovations in transportation allow us to travel around the world faster than ever, but these innovations pollute the earth.

The 1 percent of the population who has money to invest in new technology sees business profits increase and lifestyle improve, while the 99 percent of us who have only some cash get the short end of the stick most of the time. We see a chance of losing our jobs because of new technology, and this makes us wish there wasn't technology at all. In fact, we need to embrace the world of technology to stay ahead of the game. We need to make it work for us. The trick is in using the technology that we need, not the one brought to us.

Technology makes work easier; there is no doubt about it. In the twentieth century, manufacturing was sort of a gold mine for industrialized countries. Technology brought prosperity around the world and kept the United States ahead of the game. The rest of the world realized that the only way to leap ahead was by manufacturing and industrializing their main means of production. This would increase the chances of economic prosperity—by making work easier, not harder. Technology has helped reduce risk of injury, as well as improved reliability and productivity. When corporations invested with confidence in new technology—either to help them expand their business or explore new areas for business—all they had to worry about was finding people to fill new job positions. Some positions would require some expertise or considerable amounts of experience and higher education.

But then the technology sped up, and service became the main thing, hugely facilitated by the Internet. The cost of goods went up, even with China's globalization of low-priced products, and world competition intensified, mostly by technological means, where almost any job could be done with the help of technology. And it is worsening. The question then becomes, is the technological advancement continuing to help us work smarter, not harder? Of course not, and here's why:

The lucky ones who have good jobs and a helping hand from technology could think that they are working easier, but the reality is that they have to worker harder to meet the new productivity standards of the newest "toy." Anything short of that is their own fault, which means they had better give what is expected of them. If you don't want to stand in the unemployment line, stretch your knowledge and skills to meet the requirements of new technology. Actually, you'd be better off to exceed those requirements, even if you have to upgrade your skills through night courses. I will say, then, that technology makes work smarter but harder.

But issues with technology don't stop there. While it brings so many goodies, it also brings destruction. As of now, you can carry your entire life in a smartphone, watching the action of the world as it unfolds, no matter where you are or where the event is happening. You can have a surgery performed by a surgeon robot that is smarter than humans, or jump in a car and let the computer take you to wherever you want to go. But technology also has a lot to do with the worldwide unemployment and its catastrophic economic effect. And it doesn't stop there.

Technology is sucking the life out of our family values, traditions, and culture. My son William and his girlfriend, Tiffany, came over one Saturday. During the time we were talking, William's phone vibrated a couple of times, and he checked it each time. That interrupted the conversation, even though he didn't actually answer his phone. Or how often have you been sitting at dinner while someone at the table was sending text messages? And maybe details of the meal later were posted on Facebook.

This type of communication takes away the quality face-to-face conversation. You may like it that way, but when you go to job interviews, you have to know how to speak face-to-face.

We now stand in the middle of the technology aisle, full of toys that will make us stronger or help our workload, or that serve no purpose other than entertainment, and kill certain types of communication. It is up to you to use your head to stay alive. Pick what is good for you and leave the rest. By that I mean that you should use your GPS only when you must, so you don't hinder your natural sense of navigation. Assure yourself that you will not get something just because it's modern and cool; get something because it makes your life easier.

13

Finances

IT IS NEVER TOO EARLY to learn about finances. It is ludicrous that we give great attention to the power of numbers and forget to teach finance. We graduate high school and step blindly into the world of money, making all kinds of mistakes because we lack the basic understanding of money and money management. We should learn finance with addition, subtraction, division, and multiplication in school. Also, instead of waiting until we move to higher education or some financial disaster wakes us up, we should start managing our simple finances by age fourteen, and by age twenty-one, we should take finances as a matter of life or death.

I believe that the lack of deep understanding of finances is a major reason why businesses get into financial trouble. I also believe that the lack of basic understanding of money management brings financial stress to people. If we taught business basics in lower levels of education, the world wouldn't suffer so much catastrophic financial devastation. And I am almost certain that if there were education and financial stability, the world would be such a beautiful place.

The twenty-first century came and extended global marketing prosperity. The media became the main channel for visualization of lifestyle, culture, nutrition, religion, and philosophical principles of people around the world.

Then the Internet spread its power; entertainment gained a new dimension, and it quickly pushed aside traditionalism, replacing it with contemporary freedom of speech and expression. The video gaming industry crashed other sectors of technology—and continues to do so—and dominated the markets worldwide at almost lightning speed with addictive games.

In the United States in 2012, about eight out of a hundred people nationwide were not working, and one in five lived below the poverty line. Yet we still have a pair of sneakers that costs $149.99. Sure, money needs to be spent to improve the economy but not to that extent. It's impossible for the 99 percent to stay within their budget, never mind have a surplus for spending and savings, and there is no sign of quick recovery of the world's economy. We understand globalization, and we know prosperity. But what kind of prosperity is this?

The Chain-Reaction Effect

Finance is hugely affected by the world's economic chain reaction, thanks to globalization and other smart economic stunts pulled by humans and nature. An economically stable world means low prices of goods and services, low unemployment, and high consumer confidence. On the other hand, whenever something goes wrong anywhere, your finances are affected in one way or another. Peace in the Middle East means the gas supply is constant and the price is low at the gas stations. Stocks go up; your investment and savings grow. When there are rumors that the relations between Iran and Iraq, India and Pakistan, China and Japan, North Korea and South Korea, Israel and Palestine, Russia and the United States, or China and the United States, are about to become ugly or that any two countries are about to be in conflict, panic visits those who invested heavily in oil, and they demand price increases. Supply becomes insufficient, price per barrel goes up, and we pay more at the gas stations and to stay warm and be nourished. When crooks on Wall Street get caught or some country needs a bailout, everybody loses some cash. When there are torrential rains, tornadoes, tsunamis, volcanoes, and other natural disasters, the whole world is affected. When the rain is enough, crops are strong, and the harvest is abundant. Then prices at the grocery stores are low. When crops are not strong, the price of gas goes up, grocery prices go up, unemployment rises and lasts longer, raises are put on hold, stocks go down, your investment shrinks, and people become stressed out. Road accidents increase, insurance premiums go up, health costs rise and coverage diminishes, plane fares increase, and even the cost of doing the laundry goes up—one quarter will give you eight minutes at a self-service laundry instead of the usual twelve minutes. Worst of all is that here, we can't control the chain reaction. All we can do is manage our money wisely so we can keep our heads above water, which happens to be a tough task, because in addition to the punches from the world's crazy chain-reaction, we have to deal with the intruders of life.

The Intruders

Intruders come unannounced to disrupt our financial control and bring frustration to our lives. And the sad part is that we can't stop them; we have to learn to live with them.

What are the intruders in life? You get a speeding ticket, or a tire blows out on the highway, or teens vandalize your car, or you get in a car accident and are a victim of hit-and-run, or a family member passes away. Maybe the parking lot at your apartment building is full, and the only parking spot is on the street, a hundred yards from your doorstep. You might oversleep because the alarm didn't go off, and so you are late for work. When you go to your car, there's a ticket on the windshield—a parking violation with a fifty-dollar fine. You trip, fall, and break an ankle. These are needs-intruders. These kinds of intruders are difficult, because you have to take care of them right away.

Wants-intruders, however, are the intruders that basically you create. They are all the purchases you make because you see something that you like—say, a sweater—and decide to buy it; or you grab last-minute items as you wait in line, such as a pack of gum, a Snickers bar, or a bag of chips. And there you go! The money meant for the electric bill is spent on a sweater you don't really need, and part of lunch money for your kids is spent on junk food.

Then there are the intruders of the heart, such as buying Christmas and birthday presents for kids. It's hard not to buy for kids, but even small plastic toys can cost nearly ten dollars. If you have numerous nieces and nephews, a big chunk of your money will go to this intruder.

Everywhere we turn and whatever we do, we find intruders of some kind. They play a big role in our lives and bring no relief to our budget and finances. On top of that, many aspects of life make the matter worse. One of them is disrespect for money.

Respect for Money

You don't want to be a cheap sucker who drives an old and discolored car that's held together by a pair of bungee cords, whose clothes are from discount stores, and who starves to death while having three-quarters of a million dollars in the bank. That is bad for you because you have no life and bad for the world's economy because you don't spend your money. At the same time, you don't want to eat at fancy restaurants every week, drive an expensive sports car, and wear only designer clothing, and then have to collect cans under the moonlight to earn the twenty bucks to pay back the money you borrowed from your girlfriend. You don't want to get thousands back on your tax return and then spend it on booze, strip clubs, casinos, and scratch tickets—and then have to come up with excuses for your buddies from whom you've borrowed money. This shows you have absolutely no respect for money. And this brings us to the relationship between your personality and a disrespect for money.

Females, for example, are born with a taste for spending. Then they might be raised in a culture that embraces spending. To make matters worse, females, in general, don't care about how much they spend on an item—that's a disrespect for money. They might make ten dollars per hour but buy a pair of shoes and jeans for eighty dollars or more. Under these circumstances, it doesn't matter how much you make; your finances will still be a mess. Even when you have a surplus in your budget, it will be negative at the end of the year because you disrespect money.

Spending for your wants-intruders could increase in a variety of ways. Jewelry, for example, is worn by women of almost all classes and races, as it gives new dimension to their beauty, and they adore jewelry. For men, wearing jewelry symbolizes flamboyancy and cultural fashion, with a great distinction in black culture. But the aspects of life that make our wants-intruders go crazy don't stop here. In fact, one of the big ones is sports-intruders! Fanatic fans see big chunks of their cash going to jerseys, hats, and other sports-related expenses. Their wants-intruders could easily chew up thousands of dollars from their bank accounts every year for the teams they support. Be a fan, but watch your finances first!

Living in a world dominated by advertisements and spending hypnotism, reckless spenders see their money vacuumed left and right, mostly by wants-intruders. There's no way they can have a working budget and finance plan. The bad part is that their lives will be dominated by intruders, and no matter how much money they have, they will always be in financial trouble, as their disrespect for money has made them a lover of wants-intruders. If they live a life they can't afford, they'll end up in debt forever and possibly homeless.

The rest of us in the 99 percent, even though we highly respect money and try to stay ahead of the needs-intruders and control wants-intruders, we still have finance migraines that make us go in circles, trying to find some fast cash to take care of the needs-intruders.

Credit Cards

I like to refer to credit cards as an uncle who is there for you when things are rough and you need financial support. He gives you a new character and identity and introduces you to his brothers, who will welcome you. How generous! But this generosity is accompanied by a long list of agreement terms and conditions in fine print that state what Uncle Plastic needs for assurance of returned favors. Once you follow the agreement accordingly, you and Uncle Plastic will live happily ever after. When you don't follow it, Uncle Plastic will start the train of chaos, and you'll be forced to ride. If you don't find a way to stop it before it arrives at the destination, you will crash and burn badly. You will have a new character and identification spelled out in some ugly words like *delinquent*. The words about your new identification will be spread worldwide quickly. You will not like it at all. In fact, you will wish you could get your hands on Uncle Plastic to teach him a thing or two, but unfortunately, it would be waste of time, because Uncle Plastic has a long line of local, state, and federal watchdogs. And you should understand Uncle Plastic's position. You see, the beginning of almost everything is full of innocence, simplicity, peace, trustworthiness, balance, and harmony. Everybody is part of one big family, where love and care is always within arm's reach. If a member falls, all the rest come to offer help and support. Every day is paradise because paradise is all it is. The evolution/revolution of things and creatures doesn't stop here or end any time soon. So no matter how powerful our wishes are that good people and things stay the same, the devil always finds a way to destroy peace and harmony and turn the paradise into hell. Uncle Plastic knows that.

It has been thousands of years since business has been done in its most simplistic and trustworthy way. In fact, business transactions were not even business by today's definition. If you had something to trade, you would leave it at the market and pick what you needed in exchange.

I don't know when the mistrust got here, although I know it was brought by Lucifer. It has been with us for the longest time, and it follows us everywhere. In business, it keeps on taking gigantic leaps. There are treaties between countries worldwide, rules and regulations in each country, and agreements between people as strategies to make business fair and square. It's an endless battle that must be fought until a miracle happens. Maybe in centuries to come, business will be fair and square. Until then, we have to deal with what we have. It's not pretty, but that's all we have. Uncle Plastic knows that too.

As the market expands globally, with more variety of products offered by many competitors, the chase of the customer's dollar becomes intense. Vendors, always challenging each other with advertisements and best products, keep business innovation always on the move. Do you think

Uncle Plastic knows that? That's one of the reasons Uncle Plastic decided to show his face to everybody instead of playing with the big boys only, as he did in the fifties. Otherwise, he'd stay behind the game, and that's not a good position. And as you see, Uncle Plastic has been around for a long time, watching things unfold to make sure he makes the right moves on the chessboard all the time. It would be foolish to be mad at him, because you are the only one to blame for your madness. Uncle Plastic tells you that he will be there for you under certain conditions, which you accept, and he will warn you about late fee charges and annual percentage rate increases. You will screw yourself up, but you don't want to do that. So let's look into why you mess up and take measures to ensure that you don't mess up, because you almost can't live without Uncle Plastic.

Why You Mess Up

Some of the great benefits of having a relationship with Uncle Plastic are financial support and a credit score. When you need a new piece of furniture, dining set, kitchen appliance, or car down payment, and things are tight, you rely on Uncle Plastic for help. This kind of transaction is a good investment—money well spent that also adds up few good points to your credit score, assuming that you don't default on payments.

Intruders, disrespect for money, and especially the power to buy with plastic can mess up our lives as they throw off our budget and disrupt our financial world. We get overwhelmed by the power to buy and forget about our power to pay, and before we know it, we're in a credit card financial mess.

As you slash your weekly checks for rent or mortgage, utilities, food, car payments, gas, and clothing, among other financial responsibilities, there will not be much left for Uncle Plastic. You tell yourself, "I'll make a payment on my next check." And that is fine, except life could play a trick on you through a needs-intruder—say the engine overheats, and your car stops far away from home because the water pump is gone. The two hundred dollars you were going to pay Uncle Plastic next week is used for the towing and repair costs. And who knows—you could use Uncle Plastic for a rental car while your car is in repair. A week goes by, you finally get your car back, and your mind is at peace. Suddenly, you remember that you did not pay Uncle Plastic yet. You check the due date, and it's past due. You call Uncle Plastic, explain your good intentions, and beg for mercy. But you got a break on the first offense. Now it's time to pay for the crime. You just made Uncle Plastic happy, as the fees and penalties of no-compliance is applied to your account. Some uncles charge thirty-five dollars as a late-payment fee. Uncle Plastic is smiling now, while you prepare yourself for the long-lasting pain of a stain on your record sheet that Uncle Plastic shares with his brothers, sisters, and friends. Of course it hurts; just don't sweat it too much.

You're not alone. This reality touches almost all of us using plastic. We try not to lean too far over the edge, but when it happens, we know that it's almost impossible not to be hit. The whip, sooner or later, will hit hard enough to bruise the back. If you can't avoid the whip, take the bitter experience as a lesson learned and proceed with caution, so you don't ever get whipped again. The following tips should help you stay trouble-free in plastic world.

- Avoid using plastic for everyday expenses. If it wasn't for intruders, we wouldn't have financial problems, because we would know what our expenses are for the week, month, and year and take measures to make sure we cover the expenses, and we wouldn't have beefs with Uncle Plastic—at least there would be less chance for that. So it is clear that intruders are responsible for most of our financial trouble. And to minimize trouble, avoid using plastic for little things, especially when you have cash available.

- Pay before you buy, the day you buy, or put the cash aside in an envelope you label "credit cards." Put the cash you would give the store cashier in there. When it comes time to make your monthly payment to Uncle Plastic, grab the cash in the envelope and make a payment. But once you have cash available, the most effective way is to pay the day you charged something and stay worry-free.

Some people say the best way to avoid late payment is paying the week you receive the bill.

- Due dates: Payments by mail sound old-fashioned now, but they are still accepted by all uncles. If you use this method, send your payment at least seven days before the due date to allow enough time for travel and processing of your check or money order. Remember to allow for weekends and national holidays when mailing a payment. Most uncles accept payments by phone and online. Either one can save you from getting in trouble with late payments, but you still must play smart with regard to due date. Here's what I mean: say your Internet isn't working, so your only choice is to pay by phone. Some uncles charge a fee for payments over the phone. It is still a good idea to use it, considering the damages that would go to your credit if you paid late. What you must not do is rely on speed services such as express mail and express payment to pay at the last minute. Things out of your control could make it impossible for you to access those services.

- Avoid canceling credit cards. Canceling cards damages your credit score and history. Ask a banker or financial advisor about this.

- Periodic zero interest: This comes from Uncle Plastic's brothers and sisters. They've heard about you and decide to befriend you with a better initial offer by charging you zero interest for few months. In this case, as long you make payments on time, you win double; you earn yourself a good score, and pay zero interest. Bad news comes when you default on your payments. On top of all the other damages, all the breaks you had are your charges now.

- How many is too many? More than one is too many. But first things first: if you can't buy with cash, don't apply for store credit. No matter how great the benefits seem to be, be firm in saying "no thanks" and walk away. All the responsibilities attached to store credit are the same or worse than regular credit card companies. One credit card is very easy to manage, and you earn all the benefits. Three or four help you build a credit score quicker but require caution because delinquency damages will be greater, and unless your balance is one-third or less than your total credit you will be in bad standing. I consider more than three credit cards too many. If the charge on each one of them is four thousand dollars or more, trouble could be right next door. Before you know it, you're paying two hundred dollars on plastic interest every month while your income stays the same. That spells trouble.

- Vacation warning: when you go away for a week or two, make sure you take care of business before you leave. Here is an example for you: A few years ago, I went on vacation overseas for two weeks. I used a couple of credit cards to buy gifts and a few items to be resold during my vacation, thinking that the profits would go toward paying the plastic. Before I left home, I did my best to leave things under control—no bills that couldn't wait until my return. When I returned home, things were lagging, and I had to move quickly to catch up. The charges I'd made on my cards—the items I'd intended to sell with the intention of making profits and paying plastic back—was a bad idea, because I'd sold nothing. I'd thought I'd left things under control—until I checked the messages on the answering machine and opened the mail and realized I was faced with increased debts with Uncle Plastic, delinquency on my records, increased APR, late-fee charges, and on and on.

So when you go on vacation, make sure you pay all your bills, especially the ones to be due in a week or so. In case you can't make it back home according to your plans, you have some time to take care of business. And if you use plastic to go on vacation and during your vacation, make payments as soon you return. The vaccine for financial trouble is a budget.

Budget

I think finance is about budgeting, and a budget is about expenses that you must take care of on a monthly basis, such as rent or mortgage, car payments, insurance, gas, food, or utilities. There are other needs and wants that could fall into weekly expenses as well. All can fit into one budget that includes taking care of immediate and long-term expenses.

In a chaotic economic world like this one, your skills in managing your money become your only reliable friend and force you to understand and respect the simple rule of economic life: live within your means. If you make a thousand dollars a month, make sure you spend less than a thousand dollars a month. Those who became financially successful applied living within their means and respect for money principles early in their lives, but that doesn't mean you can't get your financial house in order because you didn't do the same. You are going to take matters in your own hands, and a budget is your first step. And since intruders can't leave us alone, the best remedy for them is preparedness. Include them on your budget or put some cash aside to cover expenses out of your budget.

Have a notebook to log every single expense not in the budget for at least a couple of years. That will not be easy in the beginning, but as long as you keep doing it, it will eventually become habit. After a couple of years of monitoring intruders, you'll have a pretty good idea of what should go to the intruders. It doesn't hurt to add a couple of hundred dollars to whatever number you get. Now you make your budget. Whatever the monthly amount that goes to intruders, stick with it to your best ability.

Don't panic when you spend three times the allowance. Take a closer look at where the money went. If you bought stuff you had to buy, then there is nothing you can do about it, other than being mad because your budget is off. Try to compensate in the months to come by not responding to intruders of wants. That's about it.

You add all your income to see if you make enough. Instead of spending your entire surplus, spend some, and save the rest. Spending all of it is bad, because when intruders knock on your doors, you will have nothing to rely on, and saving all of it is bad because you don't help the economy, and you don't enjoy life.

If you have just enough to cover your expenses, you are in trouble. There is no way that intruders will leave you alone. When they knock, unless you are prepared, they knock out your budget and disturb your finances. So take necessary measures, such as sacrificing some needs and most wants. Examine your budget to find what you can eliminate, or prepare yourself to borrow cash.

After you have your budget up and running, you have the real work of finance: staying in control.

Staying in Control

One of the easy ways to keep your budget in control is by having cash available for the entire monthly expenses, and that includes intruders. You distribute it according to your budget and replace that money with your weekly checks. This way, you won't have to worry about something being left behind for the next month or next check. Create a portfolio with individual folders for each item. I use blank envelopes—one for rent, one for insurance, one for car payments, one for gas, one for cable, one for cell phone. Organize your bills in a way that your weekly check will cover the entire weekly expense. This is a simplistic way of having a budget and keeping it under control. It works for me, but that doesn't mean it will work for you, and you can create your own style of budget or ask for help from professional financial advisors. Once you have a budget, follow it and create ways to improve your financial life, focused on living right today and having a better tomorrow.

The Future

Finances get complicated by a number of things we have no control over, and in a lot of cases, there is not much we can do to change its course. We shouldn't hope that we all live happily as rich brothers and sisters, because we are not created to live like that. Every day, we search for ways to distinguish ourselves from our brothers and sisters and old school friends. In every game there must be winners and losers, so the game can be interesting. Economically speaking, the game has always been won by the small number of players, which now has reached the very low mark of 1 percent.

Economy and finances are similar to body and soul—one takes the punch, the other feels the pain; one coughs, the other catches the flu. Future economy has a rougher road ahead, despite the potential we have now. It seems that the problem is us. We refuse to accept it; we deny it more strongly each day. We have created problems that are almost impossible to fix—either we don't know how, or we don't care. We know that the financial, educational, and lifestyle inequality can't go on, but we turn around and make it better for the 1 percent and worse for the 99 percent. We don't search to find out what we have become and then change course. Under this condition, our finances don't stand a chance to shine flamboyantly tomorrow.

What we need to do is take necessary measures now. This should be enough reason to learn how to have stable finances, regardless of your personality and economic power. Looking at the future with less chance for prosperity doesn't necessarily mean being pessimistic. It means that we understand the dynamics and are taking responsibility for succeeding tomorrow, no matter how it comes to us, by taking care of it today.

Technology will continue to make life easier and richer for those already rich, but it will worsen economic and social inequalities, leave more people jobless, and bring more financial chaos. Don't wait until hopelessness embraces you before you take action. Start working at things today to avoid being a victim of a tougher tomorrow. And here's the beauty: if tomorrow happens to be prosperous, you, the guy who prepared for a bad tomorrow, will win double. I recommend that you gear up for a tougher future, regardless.

Time comes that we have to see the future. Not in the way prophets do but by piecing things together, by analyzing historic events of human intelligence. We have come a long way but have much longer to go! Having come this far, we can't stop evolving. All we can do is use our brains to prepare for the storm.

We had the best of life a long time ago. Now, we are headed to chaos and destruction. We had bad things in the past but not as bad or dramatic. Natural disasters, crooks, and politics—we found them here, we grew with them, we'll die, and they will live. As we mess with nature more, we get whipped more often and drastically. As population increases, our living resources will decrease and human barbarity and other problems will diversify and multiply. Ever since the invention of machines, people saw them as threats to employment. Now they have become more sophisticated and replace a greater number of workers. Then the computer came to make matters a hundred times worse.

Every new technology comes to make people's lives easier and more interesting, but the cost of the side effects are not pretty. Here is an example of "too much of a good thing is bad for you." Technology puts more cash in the pockets of the few (1 percent) and sucks up the money of the majority—another way for rich to be richer and poor to be poorer. I see no change on this trend.

I believe that an optimistic attitude about a pessimistic future calls our attention to our finance and budget in a sense that we spend what we must spend on needs, drastically reduce spending on wants, and save some for tomorrow. I also hope that it awakens our ability to understand the need to introduce finances in all levels of education, so the children—carriers of the torch to the next generation—will have better luck. It is important that we and the future generations are rich.

Money Is an Evil Thing; It Doesn't Buy Happiness

Poor people, those most in need of money, are the ones victimized by the myth that money is an evil thing, the root of all evil. Culture and religion play a big role here. I grew up hearing, inside and outside of churches, that rich people wouldn't go to heaven, because Jesus said that it would be easier for a camel to go through the eye of a needle than for the rich to reach the reign of God. So I grew up wanting to go nowhere except heaven, until I gave my own interpretation to that message and realized that I can be rich and stand as good a chance to go to heaven as poor people. I still want to go there, except I don't care as much if I end up somewhere else. As a matter of fact, there were times that lack of money whipped me so harshly that I would have done anything to ease the pain and not cared about going somewhere else. I know now that many people misunderstood the message and took it to mean that it is better to suffer and die poor than to be filthy rich, because that is the ticket to heaven. They may be right, but I also know that money could be the last item on the list of things that could stop you from getting to heaven, while your devilish actions could be on the top of the list. I sense that if you use the money for good causes, you give God no reason to be unfair to you. In fact, I heard that God blesses the money of those who have it and curses those who don't have it. I don't get this coming from God, but I guess what it means is that you should try to understand and love rich people, instead of wishing you could spit on their faces and avoid them, because you smell the ashes of hell when you stand close to them. When we say "money doesn't give you happiness," we are generalizing the evil actions of some of those who are rich, mostly motivated by greed.

It could be that you were born with a broken wooden spoon in your mouth. Obviously, you worked hard to earn yourself the silver spoon you now have, and you look at them with pride. I respect you for that. But you are now dominated by the daunting power of money that apparently has sucked you into its devilish level, the one I call loss of integrity. At no time are you forced to face the next level, the one I call disclosed greed. Here, you have enough to go around, but you can't see it because you are consumed by greed. You look only at opportunities to increase what you have by whatever means within your powers. Your definition of life now is all about you and how much money you have. Forget decency, principles, and all that you now call crap. Money is all that matters to you. And that attitude takes you to the danger zone—the power of destruction. Here, you eliminate your competitors from the game by using rules of unfair gaming, tricks, and plots. You are screwing everybody. You've become one of the black-hearted with money, carrying a double-edged sword and looking for opportunities to slice and dice. It's just a matter of time before stress, depression, or an enemy's revenge puts your lights out. If this describes you, money does not buy happiness.

Happiness is not having everything. We know that. We also should know that if money can't give us most of what makes us happy, nothing can. I am positive that women, loving money the way they do, wouldn't have a problem finding happiness whenever there's a lot of money. For example, if shopping and partying with plenty of sex doesn't bring them happiness, then nothing can. They see money and happiness as inseparable twins (me, too). They don't see any evil thing connected to money (me, either!). It is undeniable that once we have created what constitutes happiness in our heads, money will help us build that castle that comes with living in a style and standards unique to our dreams and desires. Money will get us into the best school, allow us to have the best health care, vacation in whatever exotic places we choose, drive the best cars and fly first class, and even have a lover of our dreams. It also allows us to give the same to those we care about. I am sure that most of us would choose to die from something stupid caused by money abundance than to die of starvation and painful disease due to lack of money. So yes, money does buy happiness. You just need to shop right. People without money and zero possibility of having tons of it are the first to stand to the false statement that money is an evil thing and that it doesn't buy you happiness. Don't tell me that! We are born with a taste for money, and I believe that we shouldn't mess with our born desires.

Abundance Is a Good Power

Even as children, we understand the importance and power of money. We don't know how it drives the markets and our lives, but we know that there is a connection. We all remember kids holding dear to money and how quickly they realized that more of it is always better. One way they know the power of the money is by watching people shopping; for a little bit of things, you pay a little bit of money, and for a lot of stuff, you pay a lot of money. It then sinks in that the more stuff you want, the more money you will need to pay.

I will never forgot how my son acted after I told him I had no money. He went right to my legs, checked one and then the other, and grabbed my wallet. I was hiding it from his mom, but he found it!

As we grow older, we understand that money is the magic reality that we need for survival. Without it, we live a sad and painful life of starvation, homelessness, and deprivation of most of the fun and interesting things life has to offer. So don't be afraid of money. Have lots of it, and indulge in it. Just understand the reasons behind the myth and avoid the traps. I am relying on the wisdom granted to me by God to do good—for myself and for others—and I am sure that having a lot of money will help me do better.

You must have heard that the rich are sitting on trillions of dollars, instead of putting it in the market to help the economy stand on its feet. Others say that the rich didn't want to help the economy, so President Obama would lose re-election. That could be part of the game, but I am quite confident that the main reason is the bad market. It's the responsibility of the rich to ensure that their money grows. They know that putting their money in the market of a bad economy will not make them more money. In fact, nobody, except those who think that money is an evil thing and doesn't buy happiness, will give credit to the rich who let themselves go broke. People, in general, expect the rich to keep growing their money.

Life of the Wealthy

People have wrong ideas about the life of rich people. They think that the wealthy get everything they want easily, don't have to work for anything, and don't have problems. We reveal this feeling every time that life whips us hard and we say that we wish we were rich.

The life of the wealthy is not like that. Sure, there is enough money to go around, but life doesn't come easy to anybody. In fact, the wealthy work harder, go through greater problems, and have more worries than the poor. Remember the chain reaction? The chain reaction of rich people extends from the United States to China to Japan to Russia to South Africa and back. They have to watch the work of the assembly line more carefully, and there is more hassle to fix the broken sections. You see, when you have nothing, you worry about something. When you have something, you worry about everything. There is also the connection between wealth, personality, and reputation. While poor people struggle to make money for living, rich people are working on other things beyond wealth. Personality and reputation require that they continue to make money. They have higher standards of life, and they must maintain those standards. Reputation comes along too. People expect certain behaviors from them, and they also feel the obligation to protect that reputation. Taking care of that requires making more money and the continuation of making more money. They have enough money to enjoy their lives forever, but that's not all they want. They have dreams that have nothing to do with making money, and they must work hard to make them come true, just like everybody else. Running for office is an example. They don't run to become richer; actually, they become less rich, as they waste so much money in campaigning. They lose sleep, and the stress takes ten years off their lives, but they keep going, because they know that making dreams come true comes with sacrifices proportional to the size of the dreams.

If the rich don't watch their finances like a hawk, they will go broke and die of stress, shame, and heart attack. Watching their finances is tremendous work, and they hire the best to help. This doesn't mean, though, that you should embrace the pain and suffering of poor people, especially when you have the potential to turn yourself into a rich person. So get it out of your head that the rich have no worries, hard times, and nightmares. Being rich means having almost all the necessary means to make your dreams come true, help others make their dreams come true, and make the world a better place for us and the generations to come. For all that, any sacrifice is worth the cause.

Time to Be Wealthy

It's never too soon or too late, a good time or a bad time to start working toward building your wealth. Ask people who know; they'll tell you. Read books about becoming wealthy; you'll find out.

If you start young, you will have a lifetime ahead of you to play the game over and over, until you get it right. If you start old, you can use your life experience and wisdom to avoid the falls that rookies take.

There will be many opportunities to grow your wealth. And in a world of economic uncertainty, wealth may grow at a slow pace, but as long as you continue to play your cards right, you have nothing to worry about, and when things turn around, you will be in a good position to leap.

Don't be discouraged, thinking it is impossible to be rich these days. Fight your best to get out of poverty, and accept what you get. I am sure you will like the outcome—anything is better than poverty. This attitude puts you ahead of the game. You will not fall into the trap of those in charge of the game who are cheating and changing the rules in the middle of the game—the 1 percent controlling 45 percent of total wealth, rumors say. You know that money rules and makes the game go around. I don't believe the 99 percent are happy with the way the game is going. It's your choice to refuse to stand still and be smacked around like a ping-pong ball. Show that you are a valuable player, no matter how difficult the conditions are. Learn the ways the 1 percent take, and then follow them or create a unique strategy to beat them.

Doing that puts you in a good position and gives you a competitive edge. If you have been waiting for the perfect time to begin creating wealth, the time for action has come. Take the first step today, and keep on marching with determination. I hope that you have the desire and drive to make a lot of money, no matter how young or old you are, or at least die trying to be rich.

Savings and the Power of Money

Rumors say that rich people invest their money to make it grow, and that poor people save their money to lose it to inflation. Whatever the truth might be, here's what I think: rich people save their money as well. The difference is that rich people save as a preventive measure, in case something really bad happens, and poor people save to take care of intruders and the future.

I always treated my kids with unconditional love; I think most parents do. When my son was about two and a half years old, in one of the many trips we made to the store, he saw a Power Rangers toy. He grabbed two of them right away. I told him he could have only one, but he refused to put the other one back. I snatched one out of his hands and put it back myself.

That triggered the annoying cry that made me angry but hit his mother's heart. She asked why I couldn't let him keep both toys. I explained to her that the toys were identical. I paid and left quickly to avoid more annoyance and embarrassment.

After many attempts to stop him from crying without success, I told myself that it was a game to seduce me, and that by the time we were about halfway home, he would understand that I wasn't falling for his trick and would stop crying. That proved me wrong. The crying went all the way home and continued in the living room. I became aggravated, and his mother still thought I had no reason to refuse paying for the other toy. That was making me angry too, but as I lay there on the couch, watching nothing on TV, I connected my brain to my heart and realized that my son was still upset—the other toy was something meaningful to him. Nothing mattered more than that toy he didn't have. A sense of guilt surrounded my soul and made me feel like an uncaring, unloving father. I grabbed the keys, went back for the other toy, returned home in no time, and gave him the other toy.

I was counting on a big hug, but that didn't come—at least not right away—but I knew I'd made his day, so I stayed close by to see his reaction. Soon enough, I understood the game: he needed the two toys so he could create fights between them. Watching him lost in his world of fun and imagination created one of those lifetime memories that only got better as he gave me one Power Ranger, followed by words, "Let's play, Daddy."

And there you have it: one of the intruders that required immediate attention. Twenty dollars for the two toys was nothing, but it gave me a lifetime memory, rather than regret, because I saved money for intruders. And this one happened to be a big one.

It seems that saving is one of the things that we learn to do. As soon as we begin to understand this world, we notice that our parents save. Food is probably the clearest picture. As we understand more, we realize that saving goes beyond food. What we still don't understand is why we can't all save—not just grown-ups but everybody! I started to save before anybody told me to do so. That was a long time ago.

Besides intruders, the advertisers want to turn all of us into potential buyers and spending freaks—not savers. Everybody around you spends, the Internet is helping advertisers, and your brain grows to believe that spending is fun and that saving sucks.

It is not expected that a child will understand the meaning of saving and start to save. Children don't take care of themselves; adults do. Fortunately, adults know that we should save. It is expected that we will save. We try to save. It is just that we have to take care of today before saving for tomorrow, and most of the time, today doesn't give us the break we need to save for tomorrow. Saving happens to be one of the easiest hard things to do.

Saving is care for tomorrow—the uncertainty, the thing we don't know about. We know it exists. We picture it, imagine it, create and mold it in our minds, and hope that it comes. But today must exist first and be taken care of first. Experience has shown us that taking good care of today ensures tomorrow's success. So we are conditioned to take care of today.

As we jump from being babies to children up to adults and then elderly, we understand more about life at each phase, and we learn the meaning of saving. Some of us pick that up ourselves, and the rest of us fall into the culture: parents do it, friends do it, governments do it, everybody does it, and life proves to you that it should be done. You definitely want to save and stay the course. Taking care of today, however, which is becoming impossible for the 99 percent, is hurting the chances to save. We could call this a depression or depression's second blow. The saving reality we are left with is this: as soon as we get it going, an intruder comes along to make us use the savings or sometimes wipe it all out. We start out again from scratch, and months later we see it shrinking or stagnating. It's very discouraging, but not saving at all is asking for trouble. That's why we are going to the streets in protest. We know that we must save, and we can't keep going without the possibility of saving. I don't believe we have the solution for the problem, but by going to the streets, we are at least telling the ones in charge to find solutions.

By the time a child reaches grade three, he or she should have a good understanding of saving and begin to do it. At this age, we don't earn to save, of course, but we get an allowance for the little work we do around the house, such as vacuuming our room, scrubbing the tub for Mommy, or cleaning Daddy's car. Fifty cents here and a dollar there could go to our savings piggy bank.

Besides intruders, the advertisers want to turn all of us into potential buyers and spenders. As a child, growing up under a bombardment of ads, it becomes impossible not to fall. Your brain grew with a belief that spending is fun. Everybody around you spends, and the Internet is doing a good job of turning you into spending freaks; you just can't hide. The real meaning of saving—to protect, not to destroy—is left behind, and its principle is lost in translation.

Let's see the truth behind small savings: almost everybody can save five dollars per week. That equals $260 a year and $2,600 in ten years. Not much, so you don't care. But watch things turn around: if you start that saving at age eighteen, by the time you are sixty-eight, you will have thirteen thousand dollars. Some of us might say, "How old do I think I am, five? That's fifty years of saving five dollars weekly. Inflation makes that stupid five dollars worth nothing." Sure! That's why most of us don't save, because we can only save so little, and the inflation will kill it. It could be true, technically, but I want you to focus on the beautiful side of the pie: thirteen thousand dollars is thirteen thousand dollars, anywhere and at any time. I bet you that many of those at age sixty-eight are pulling their hair for not having saved that stupid five dollars a week from the age of eighteen. Thirteen thousand would put a smile on their faces. The other good reason is that when you understand the principle, you will get to the point where you want desperately to see the number growing. You have reached one grand; now you can't wait to see fifteen hundred, two grand, ten grand, and you are seriously determined to grow your money.

Small savings get you to the principle of saving, and once you get the groove going, it's only excitement from there. I remember a story of a woman who saved lunch money, bus fare, and so on and became a millionaire. If there is one case I know, I imagine there are many more. Remember: to be big, you must start small—even life teaches you that. "A drop here, a drop there, and before you know it, it's a flood." Here you have some examples of those small drops. And the secret is to never stop that savings from growing; that is, never touch it unless you can touch it to make it grow faster.

And this type of saving is not the kind we have in a bank or under the mattress that we use to cover emergencies. This is the long-term saving—the one we decide to save until we retire. In fact, it makes sense that we start small. This way, it will not affect our finances to the point that we'll have to reduce or stop saving.

Compound interest is interesting. A five-dollar saving, when it reaches impressive numbers, opens opportunities to make more money. Even leaving it to multiply with interest and other ways to grow your untouchable savings account, such as investments, could take care of you when you can no longer work. The problem is that in the duration, the greed and urge to live a full life today make it so discouraging to have a longtime untouchable account. Think outside the box, or at least save for the sake of saving—a little, a lot, whatever you can.

To have your finances under control is to have your life under control. When you have your life under control, you stand ahead of the game. To be ahead of the game, you must know how to play the game—the game of self-control for financial control. First, you must understand and respect financial control. Second, you must learn the basics of organized finances and adopt a system that works for you. Third, educate and empower yourself to resist the hypnotism of advertisement and all other sorts of games out there designed to suck up your money, drain your savings, throw you out of the game, and leave you in financial mess. You might be one of those people who can't manage money correctly. There are lots of types of financial help available at no charge.

Any time you feel the temptation to stop saving, remember that you must share what you have with tomorrow, today. Tomorrow is the time that you can no longer produce as today, but you still must live, and living in tomorrow is more demanding than living today.

Saving for tomorrow, today, puts you ahead of tomorrow's game.

14

Drugs, Alcohol, Cigarettes, and Prostitution

Drugs

DRUGS ARE THE SALVATION FOR many but the destruction for a much larger number worldwide. For those using their heads, it's a benefit, but it's a dangerous way to destroy lives for those who become hooked.

Just as everything else in life, good and bad are inseparable, with one of the two dominating. Look at us! We are the complex mix of viruses, germs, and bacteria—good and bad. When good ones win, we're fine; when not, we're sick. In the drug world, the good is losing. The power of destruction tips the balance of success, and the youth are hit the hardest.

There are different levels of calamity and dangerous wealth potential, with drug lords on the throne, in charge of high transactions done by powerful means of negotiation and confirmed by trusted service men who will travel in private jets to seal the deal at remote places.

The next level below, in charge of turning the merchandise into fabulous cash, is where the action lives. The promotion to good performers and the catastrophic measures taken with snitches, bad dealers, cheaters, and self-consumers all happen here. So when you are requested to report to the office, your heart rate is the highest of all time, because you never know where the first swing will come from.

As you walk in, you look at your buddies standing across the room, dressed in black and gray, with shiny black shoes, legs spread about a foot apart, hands held in front of their crotches, and wearing dark sunglasses. They are the loyal dogs who protect their lord and carry out orders from their superiors. You don't greet them, because you will not be greeted back. You know that. You also know that punishments are not carried out in the big office, unless the crime is extreme and demands immediate resolution. So that could give a chance of coming up with some kind of escape plan as soon as you clear the room.

As you get tapped on the face by the open hand of the boss, you remember what happened to your cousin Vinny, and your imagination runs wild. You start to sweat heavily, but after few minutes of serious conversation, you are let go. That's like a miracle!

That was too good to be true, so as you walk out, your worries and fear kick in. You haven't felt this frightened in a long time. You reach your car and release the hood latch to check under the hood for something suspicious. Your fears somewhat vanish. You start the car—it didn't explode! It's running! You drive away, vowing not to screw up again. But your fear comes back. As you move on the road, so does one blue SUV, and it's taking all the turns you take. The next set of lights is approaching. You know a shortcut—you take it, and the SUV takes it too. At the first chance, you pass the car in front of you. The SUV is now second behind you. Suddenly, it turns right and drives away.

You make it to your driveway. You are almost safe. Once in the house, you look around for something misplaced or odd. You check the microwave, smoke alarm, closet, and bathroom. You walk up to the living room window, still looking for something, but you see nothing. You grab a can of Budweiser and sit on the couch. You reach into the right pocket of your blue jeans to grab a small wrapped item and throw it on the table. You pull out a cell phone and dial some numbers.

You don't remember being angry with your underlings in a long time. Suddenly, out of fear of your life, you are laying out death threats to them. If things don't improve, you are fucked. That cannot happen. You don't want to be the one to be found behind a Dumpster with a smashed skull and broken bones. No more Mr. Nice Guy. "Take care of business" is the ultimatum you give them. And they'd better warn the corners.

Every business carries risks. Some are easily manageable, others are a lifetime search for solution. The drug business carries the same common risks … plus one—the deadly risk. The lower your rank, the higher the chances of something going terribly wrong.

The lowest end of the drug industry is the consumer. He simply wants to have enough cash to support his unfortunate habit. Of course, he wishes he could step up into the house, because there, even though there are dangerous games, he would be on the top of the world. Business transactions are in the millions, you live a life larger than life, including the abundance of cash. You cruise in a black Mercedes-Benz with tinted windows, live in a mansion with a pool, and are surrounded by women. There are Swiss Bank accounts under fake names and the best protection for you and your family. There is, of course, one clear and present danger, which is an endless war to fight, but that's part of the game. But you know you stand no chance. So the choice is to lay low on the streets, always look out for cops, and stay under cover.

Despite the abundance, the price goes up every day. Consumers' buying power diminishes, and the addiction becomes life-threatening. Desperate measures are often taken, and tragedy strikes every day—an overdose takes innocent young lives.

The lucky ones, probably not badly addicted, manage to hold a job at some fast-food restaurant or warehouse, or in landscaping, construction, painting, or carpentry, making just enough to cover for whatever their basic and drug needs are.

The others in the same situation but not in control of the cash run out of cash for drugs and turn themselves into a consumer/dealer, stretching the dollar farther than it can go. When this strategy proves unreliable, which it does in most cases, they move to dealer/consumer. The merchandise is now stretched instead of the dollar, so there will be leftover for self-puffing and sniffing.

As long as the payments are kept on time and according to the agreement, there is nothing to worry about, but when you are short of cash and merchandise, trouble knocks loud on your doors. Usually, you get a warning for the first offense, but you are ordered to have the cash ready for the next collection date and warned never to be late or short again. It could be a good idea to obey the order and avoid dodging the bullets. From here, you move to robbery at gas stations and convenience stores for fast cash, or you hit banks' small branches. Women often turn to prostitution to make up for a shortage of cash.

Male or female, regardless of how you get cash for your drugs, sooner or later those means will bring you regretful pain. And remember that getting cash for drugs is not the biggest problem; handling a drug problem is. You hear about celebrities and young stars going through hell brought to them by drugs. Why do we fry our brains for excitement?

"Stop right there!" If you know all about the drug world and are ready to join, no matter what, you have not taken into consideration that you could be making the biggest mistake of your life. You are probably lured by what appears to be a paradise of the drug world. What you don't know is that the owners of those paradises are individuals who put two and two together and come up with 666. What can you possibly bring to that danger zone? If you think that because you are made out of steel, raised with tigers and lions, and no motherfucker will fuck you, you are dead wrong. There are battalions of snipers, navy SEALs, and Tomahawk missiles waiting for you. With some luck, you will have a peaceful arrest. If not, you will be a victim of a precipitated action of the shooter, the bite of a K-9, or just toasted.

It must be the government, your friends, parents, and this messed-up world that give you this only choice for survival, right? Let me tell you that you are dead wrong. Every time you stand up to the challenges of life, there are choices for you. There is no blaming your situation on somebody or something else. But assuming that dealing drugs is your only means to survive, keep your head straight, and don't dig in too deep. The reason why you don't want to get in deeply is that when destiny shows you the light at the end of the tunnel, getting out becomes a hard challenge. You see, each gang has its own secrets, strategy, and objectives, just like government and big business. Competition makes territorial domination the most complicated and deadly problem. Getting out means the freedom to join any gang and snitch about the way the previous gang conducts business. In the drug world, snitches take bullets and bat beatings, which are deadly most of the time.

I truly believe that "if there's a will, there's a way." It doesn't matter why you got in or how deeply and messed up you are in the drug world. If you are seriously determined to get out, you will find the strength to seek and accept help from those who can help you change the direction of your life and become a citizen of valor for you, your family, friends, and the world. That's how you count. Best of all is to resist temptation, turn around, go home, and pick up one of the many other ways to pursue your happiness. Put all your dedication into it and enjoy the way you count.

Alcohol

Alcohol blends with its partner in crime, drugs. Its accessibility and legality keep you shit-faced for much less money and trouble than being stoned. Like most drugs, alcohol is addictive. The first couple of drinks make you feel good, the next few make you smarter and more talkative than your buddies, until all of you are drunk and become ignorant and stupid.

Your organs, especially the liver and kidneys, take the real punches, having to work like a machine to break down the junk of your drinks. Fortunately, your stomach stays smarter by using the nasty and painful but effective way to save your life by sending you to the bathroom to throw up. It also tells you that you have had more than enough.

After six or eight hours of dead sleep, you are finally sober and dealing with a hangover. Maybe the pounding headache is telling you something. You are just trying hard to remember what happened last night. It could be that the only remedy for your hangover is a shot or two of your favorite drink, and you could be one of the alcoholics with multiple addictions, so after drinks to kill the hangover, you light up a cigarette.

Alcohol is not so bad, not a liver-killer, as long as we drink it wisely. As a matter of fact, it does have benefits to our health when consumed in moderation—two glasses of red wine a week. Any increase to that amount could be an invitation for trouble. Your genes, personality, available cash for alcohol, and possible drunken behavior are the most important factors in allowing or banning your drinking.

Some people drink daily at home and go to the bars every weekend to drink with friends. They try to earn the reputation of being heavy drinkers. They could spend lots of cash on alcohol without concern for any other needs. I knew of someone who spent almost twenty grand on friends at the bars. Relatives had to take him home so he wouldn't get jumped, robbed, or even killed after showing off his cash at the bar. In less than six months, he was at the mercy of his brother, because he couldn't pay the rent. These types of drinkers don't have room for love and care at home. The problems that come from here—domestic violence, child endangerment, and so on—increase the chances for restraining orders, community service and incarceration, and bring tons of stress and evil thoughts.

Some people are in control every time they are drunk, while others just lose it. A friend of mine once went to a bar and drank all night. When the bar closed, he started his car, engaged in conversation with his friends, got a ride home with them, and the next morning reported his car stolen. After a couple hours, he got a call from the police, informing him that his car was found in the parking lot, with the key in the ignition.

If you drink and then can't remember what happened by the next morning, obviously you shouldn't drink; you just can't drink! If you are one of those who empties his wallet every time he goes out drinking and returns home to start a fight for no reason, obviously you shouldn't drink; you can't drink! Do the world and yourself a favor: stay sober! And this takes us to smart drinking!

Alcohol does have some benefits; the question is how to drink smart. Smart drinking is drinking whatever you like, whenever you like, within your limit, and knowing to stop at your limit, period. When you reach your limit, the drinking is over. And just to be clear, your limit should be the point where one more drink will impair your senses. Stay away from playing the stupid games of matching drinks or having drinking contests with your friends. Some people consider drinking at home one way to drink smart. You would save money by drinking at home, and you'd not get into trouble, as you might at a bar, by arguing over sports teams. Also, your kids will love playing with you, because you will be in playing mode, with no worries or concerns—although here is where trouble could come from another angle: drinking at home to forget your troubles. This is something that I've heard people talking about since I was a boy.

I don't care what your beliefs or philosophical principles are; I can tell you with almost total certainty that destiny has power over all of us. A lot of times it cuts us with double-edged swords. We try hard to pick up the pieces that seem to be not so despicable and stay alert to the next swing, but suddenly we lose the strength to fight. We don't care anymore, obviously because nothing matters anymore. Alcohol might have ruined your life, but you have at least two ways to fight back and reconstruct: put all your effort into getting sober on your own, or go to rehab. No matter who you are or how bad you are, there is no shame. Just go.

Cigarettes

My uncle was a smoker. Just for that, I always saw him as someone special. Every time he visited us, I would find ways to sit next to him. My happier times used to be the times he asked me to get him fire, which was a burning charcoal or a small piece of burning stick from tree branches used to produce fire to cook meals. I would run to the kitchen, which was located in the backyard, get one, and run back to him. Then I would watch him bring it to the tip of the cigarette he held securely in his lips. And just like magic, the cigarette was burning—my uncle was smoking!

When he was hungry for more, he would light up another and another, without losing the fire on the last one. Sometimes he would light up the cigarette while I held the burning charcoal or the piece of burning stick in my hands, and I would still watch the ceremony in amazement. More fascinating than that was the shaking of the matchstick to put out the flame after lighting up the cigarette.

The lighter never gave me the same impressive sentiment as charcoal or a burning stick, but I always thought of it as so creative. The stinky cigarette's smell wouldn't bother me. That was, in fact, the best part. Somehow, that gave my uncle such a unique scent that, to my eyes, separated him from others and made him a very special uncle. Every chance I had, I would sit very close to him.

Due to his lack of knowledge about second-hand smoking effects, especially to kids, he would put his arm around me and pull me closer to him. That was paradise, every time! Even on hot summer nights, when the heat, roaches, and bed bugs wouldn't let us sleep, the whole family and sometimes the neighbors would sit in the front yard. Under moonlight so bright that we could see our silhouettes twice our height, we would tell and hear fairy tales until late night. I would still give my life to sit close to my uncle.

Watching smokers curving one hand to block the wind from killing the flame impressed me a lot. I still find it interesting and comical as they turn their backs to the wind and keep on trying to light up cigarettes. And then comes the moment of joy! It was a joy watching them blow the smoke away, which the wind took and danced with right in front of them before it disappeared into space. This show was more spectacular when there was a calm wind and the smoke was thick—so magical!

For that, I promised myself to be a smoker when I grew up—a promise encouraged by a few of my older friends, who were competing on smoking tricks, such as holding the smoke inside their open mouth or blowing the smoke by mouth and sucking it all in through the nostrils.

In the '70s, cigarettes in my neighborhood were considered a medicine for toothache. If you were in pain, you'd smoke one or less, and the pain would go away. If you were a smoker, you wouldn't have toothaches. Children were not allowed to use that technique, though, and to women, smoking was simply morally prohibited.

The other approach to smoking was that it was the style and symbol of high class, such as doctors, lawyers, and government representatives.

To most, it was a clear distinction. To us, it was just cool watching people smoke. We never heard of it as a stress-reliever. But cigarettes seem to have become troublesome ever since. I remember my grandpa telling us that doctors recommend to their patients not to smoke. So when I was sixteen, I tried a few smokes, making sure nobody in the house found out. By eighteen I just smoked. I was eighteen—a man, not a child—and buying my own cigarettes, but I smoked mostly at parties, clubs, or for fun with my friends.

I wanted to be special like my uncle and cool like my friends, except I wasn't either one. Cigarettes were just not for me—and I am so glad for that. I am sure many smokers have a common story about how and when they tried cigarettes.

I believe that things stared out wonderfully. The industry employed many people, paid government its share through taxes, and smokers were very pleased. But one day, the government woke up, fed up with the migraines from caring for people with cancer and other health problems caused by cigarettes and other tobacco products, and it began an investigation into the truth of the industry. It seems that the government found grounds for mistrust and proof of lies, because it filed lawsuits against the industry and won. And it is clear that the relationship began to sour, and the war between the two started its engine.

From the very beginning, cigarettes had harmful potential to kill smokers. Tobacco products have nicotine and other chemicals that give a pleasurable sensation, yet keep you hooked for life and kill you slowly. Doctors still warn their smoking patients, but it has been so cool to smoke, and people of power in the industry lied and continue to lie about addiction and other health complications related to tobacco use. Advertisers have more money, so they are still crushing government's anti-tobacco campaign. High taxes only make smokers spend more. Stiff regulations made the industry send its business to other countries, where regulations are less stiff or nonexistent.

Many people believe that the fight to eliminate cigarette use is just a game to confuse people. The way I see this crisis is that the smokers are the ping-pong ball at the table. The players are here to win. But if there isn't a ball, there will be no game! That means that smokers have to leave the room and never come back. It will be painful, but not as horrible as the smacking you have been taking, with no end in sight. If you don't leave the room, the smacking will get only harder, and you will be crushed. Take a deep breath, embrace the pain of the challenge, and begin the process of leaving the room—quit smoking.

Find a quiet place, sit alone, think about it deeply, reach to your soul, and talk to angels. Remind yourself that you came to this place because you had a purpose—a commitment to stop smoking, not for a day, not for a month, not for a year but forever. You are not here to follow the steps of your friends who have tried and failed. You are here to follow the steps of those who have said, "I am done with this shit," and never again played with cigarettes. They are not more human than you, they are not stronger than you, and they are by no means more special than you. They simply took a fair decision as a personal mandate and carried it to the end. They handed the torch to you to start a new game. You make the rules, and you are the only invincible player. That should be your first step.

Your second step should be leaving the quiet place, determined to quit smoking, once and for all. You should remind yourself that the longer the time you have been smoking, the longer it will take you to quit and the more stressful it could be. But you are not about time and difficulties; you are about the final result—smoking no more.

And consider this: if you smoke one pack a day, you puff six hundred cigarettes in a month; 7,200 in a year; 72,000 in ten years, for $180 a month and $2,100 a year—and that's $21,000 in ten years at a flat price of six dollars per pack. If you continue for another ten years—and you will increase the amount due to addiction to, say, two packs a day—you will puff 216,000 cigarettes during twenty years of smoking (72,000 first ten years + 144,000 second ten years), for $63,000 at a flat price of six dollars per pack.

I will give you some encouragement and an example of a quitting plan. Take it as a suggestion, and create your own plan.

- Calculate how much you will spend on cigarettes in three years.

- Think of something that amount could give you.
- Promise yourself to get it after you quit.
- Pick an amount you want to save from your cigarette budget (say, five dollars a month).
- Take the amount left for the cigarette budget, and calculate how many packs that gives you a month. Whatever the number is, that's what you have.
- Try this for three months. You wouldn't have saved more than fifteen dollars, and that is not much, but you gave your brain a break—worth way more than fifteen dollars.
- Now the game begins! You already tried things out, and you know what you can do. So, make a real quitting plan. I suggest cutting one pack per month. If you smoke one pack a day, that is thirty packs a month. In the first month, cut to twenty-nine packs; in the second month, cut to twenty-eight packs, and then twenty-seven, twenty-six, and so on, decreasing the amount by a pack each month.

That means you can quit smoking in two and a half years without much stress to your body and brain. I don't think this is an impossible plan, but it comes with strings attached: the intruders. Remember that intruders come unannounced to mess up our plans. When quitting smoking, the intruders will dump so much stress on you that your only refuge will be smoking a couple of more cigarettes to ease your pain. Just don't rely on it every time intruders come, because they will keep coming until you die. What you want to do is build resistance to them. Deal with them in a harsh way until they stop coming. Your power of determination helps you do that.

Quitting is a combination of whatever plan you put to work, and your determination to reach the goal. Not a single plan will bring the goal without intruders trying to attack and destroy it. You protect it by making corrections and staying the course. Once you have a strong determination to reach your goal and a clear understanding that you will have to fight tons of intruders, nothing will stop you. Tobacco advertisers can dump all they want on you, but they will never take you down. Don't just sit there, complaining that it is too hard or impossible to quit. Don't sit there and blame the government for not having done better to protect you. Don't listen to losers telling you that you will never quit—they want you to be a loser like them. Listen to those who have quit and respect your decision to quit. Fight to quit because you know that you can quit. You know that those who quit are not stronger than you are. You are going to put a plan to work and another and another, until you get what you want. You will like the new you and will be happy to show the tobacco company that you are in charge of your destiny.

Prostitution

Many things can go wrong to put a woman in a delicate social status— Social Services snatched you from your mother because she was a drug addict, and your foster mom suddenly passed away when you were only fourteen. Your friends introduced you to their friends on the streets, and you are now one big family. Your virginity didn't live to see thirteen, and you don't even remember how you lost it. From there, it didn't matter anymore. Each time after that, it became less painful and more enjoyable.

You soon realized that you had something that drives boys crazy and gives you orgasms, money, food, drink, smokes, drugs, and housing in the basement somewhere. You are your only means of survival. It's becoming your own business affair, and you are becoming an expert. It seems, then, that you became the product of your destiny. But you can change your destiny.

Ladies, you are still special, because you are what you are, but that special quality can't be seen because it is covered by many layers of shame and ugliness. Your bad habits can turn you into easy prey or cheap sexual relief, and your chances of getting infections and STDs are much higher. Your children might be taken from you—think about your little girl growing up in foster care. I can only tell you that if there is a will, there is a way.

Destiny offers bad choices, and the world we are living in makes matters worse, but there is something special within each of us, and it's much more powerful than all the evil spilled on us by destiny or other means. All we need to do is reach deep into our inner self and find that power to spring us to where we want to be and should be. Most of the time it takes lots of sacrifice to reach that power, but there are times that we must obey what we must obey to enjoy life. Never focus on the pain that is taking you there; focus on the reward waiting for you.

15

Health and Fitness

LIFE IS A CHAIN OF events. We could compare it to a large assembly line, where synchronization is essential for the assembly line performance. Good maintenance of the assembly line ensures its constant, smooth flow. We also know that some sections are more important than others and require greater attention.

The same principle applies in life. Health and fitness are the main power generators juicing the whole assembly of life. If they aren't running well, other sections will work poorly or not at all. Also, the result of human activities depends on the mental and physical states of individuals—the healthier and more fit you are, the greater your achievement potential.

Factors of life such as sleep, sex, nutrition, happiness, stress, social status, environment, economic stance, culture, tradition, opportunity, and action must work in synchronization in order for us to achieve and maintain health and fitness. Action, controlled by needs and desires, seems to be the most important of all, and it cries for our participation. We are wired to act and react by instinct and by self-awareness impulses dominated by need and desire. We are hungry, we eat; we are thirsty, we drink; we are sick, we take medications or see a doctor; we are tired, we rest; we are lonely, we find company; and so on. We understand these demands and we take action every time we face one, but we neglect action on those that we think are not important at the moment. Unfortunately, many of us take action only after the need becomes chronic.

Feeling tired all the time, muscle weakness, joint pain or discomfort, stress, and depression are clear signs that it's time to start moving. When they hit, the wheels of physical activities should start to roll. And fortunately, exercise, one of the best types of physical activities that can be done at any age, is here to keep the wheels of action spinning. That's why doctors recommend that parents keep kids active and reduce TV and video game time and that adults stay active as well. In fact, the older we are, the greater our need to exercise. And this seems to be the greatest and cheapest "prescription" doctors can offer, as there are numerous ways to exercise—playing hide-and-seek; riding a bike; playing basketball, soccer, baseball, and tennis; dancing; swimming; jogging; martial arts; boxing; skiing, gymnastics; or weight lifting.

Swimming is considered the number-one aerobic exercise, followed by dancing, since these activities bring the whole body into action. I would give weight lifting the gold medal, because I feel it is the foundation of all sports and types of physical activities. No matter what you choose, just remember to exercise before stress, depression, and obesity team up to take you down, and if you're already exercising, keep doing what you are doing.

Weight lifting is something that you can do at a fitness club, home gym, or both. Fitness clubs require sign-up fees and monthly dues, but they have many benefits, such as personal trainers, a variety of machines, tanning rooms, and special workout rooms for aerobics, cardio, kickboxing, bicycling, and treadmills. They also may have an indoor pool and tennis and basketball courts. But fitness clubs do come with inconveniences—you have to drive there; management or staff may be unprofessional or not helpful; the facility might not be clean or sanitized, or it could be too cold in winter and too hot in summer; and you have to deal with other club members, some of whom may not show common courtesy and ignore the club's rules, such as returning the weights to the rack or wiping down the equipment after use. And last but not least, there are the morons who don't know proper behavior in a gym or fitness club. They take longer than necessary on the machines, they bark loudly on their cell phones (right in front of the gym's sign: *No cell phones allowed!*), and they exhibit many other annoying behaviors that make you want to smack them. My advice to that is simple: "If you can't handle the heat, get out of the kitchen!" Use a home gym.

If you choose a home gym, you will face the pros and cons. Pros include having your gym easily accessible in your own home; you eliminate wasting time driving to the gym; you can work out alone without concerning yourself with sharing the equipment. Cons might be that you are your own incentive. No one will be there to inspire motivation and boost your desire to catch up to someone who's looking better and working out harder than you. You might miss the variety of machines a gym provides, as well as the gym's social environment—you can't make any friends in the basement. And your workout can be terminated prematurely and bothered frequently by family members or small home emergencies.

There's a third option—joining a fitness club and using a home gym. Chances are, however, that you won't have full results from either one, because you will split the schedule and come up with excuses to work at home instead of at the club. But once you understand that the best results depend on your discipline, commitment, and self-motivation, signing up for a fitness club and having a gym at home is a plus for you. Actually, when you have that type of mind-set, you can get great results from an exercise bike in your bedroom.

Working Out at Fitness Clubs or Home Gyms

Schedule: Make sure your gym schedule doesn't conflict with other important errands, such as piano lessons, basketball and tennis practice, karate, or dancing classes for your kids.

Types of schedule: Have two in, one out, two in again and two out. For example, Monday and Tuesday are for the gym. Wednesday is rest. Thursday and Friday—gym. Weekend is rest. Most gym-goers choose this schedule because it is the best, but what matters is having a weekly schedule that you can follow.

Commitment: When you feel like staying home because the weather is miserable, remember your commitment. If you have a partner, the commitment is more serious and both of you should respect it. And remember, just because your partner can't make it, it doesn't mean that you can't either. Commitment should take you there to do whatever you can by yourself.

Control: I use a notebook to write down my program and monitor my progress. Doing so stops me from trying to remember which machines I used last week and which order and what weight I had on each set. Also, I don't have to wait until I get to the gym to decide what to do.

Consistency: Work out (whether at a fitness club or home gym) at the same time all the time.

Purpose: When you start the gym, you need to know what you want out of it, so you can select machines, exercises, and the workout intensity accordingly. For example, if you joined to lose weight, your program will be different from people who joined to gain muscle.

Workout Intensity

Workout intensity depends on an individual's primary goals. Say you are a competitive sport girl. You need to maintain your feminine design but also increase your strength and endurance for the competition. Your workout intensity should be moderate overall and high for some particular body parts, pretty much the opposite of working out to lose weight, where the intensity should be high in cardio, low in weight lifting. But the bottom line for women is not to sweat it when it comes to muscle growth. Tone yourself with lightweight exercises and boost your self-esteem with cardio exercises.

For guys, the story is different. Most want to build muscle, but that doesn't mean focusing on strength training only, because then they could become a bull. And so the dominant rule for women and men is the attention to the individual's primary goals on exercise and weight lifting.

If you are bulky before you even join the gym, your focus should be on being ripped. Burn it with moderate-intensity cardio and abs. If you feel the need to gain lots of muscle, you must hit heavy lifting without underestimating cardio and abs, so you can avoid the embarrassment of benching four hundred pounds, leg pressing a thousand pounds, but only being able to jog a quarter of a mile before passing out—you are powerful but unfit.

I am only my own trainer, but I have been going to the gym for many years and achieved outstanding results. I am confident in telling you that there is no universal best formula for getting the ultimate results of working out. I am sure that individual physical uniqueness backs up my claim. Individual programs combined with the right exercises are some of the formulas that bring the best results from weight lifting. You listen to your muscles, monitor your progress, and strictly follow your plan. Stay the course if you like the results, or make corrections to your plan, adjustments to your workout, and monitor your progress. If you feel the need for help, ask, and keep monitoring your progress. If you're unsure what to do, ask someone who looks like he knows what he is doing, or hire a trainer.

You might feel uncomfortable because it's the first time you've joined a fitness club—that's normal. Little by little, you will gain confidence, and in no time, you will be as good as almost anybody.

Avoiding Injuries

Warm-up: A warm-up is a lifesaver. Always warm up before you start lifting. It doesn't matter which exercises you choose, as long they do the job. Treadmill and bicycle are the most popular. (Five to ten minutes on a treadmill with some incline and speeds up to seven is my favorite. To finish my warm-up, I do a few light shoulder-and-back exercises.)

Stretching: Stretching is very important—period. You are never too young to start, and the older you are, the more you need it. Ask martial artists, sports players, or physical therapists.

Dark clouds: No matter how well you plan and monitor your life, there will always be something coming out of nowhere—the intruders—to make you go off course. A fitness program is no exception. Eventualities that stop us from going to the gym might be a bad cold, a migraine, or a serious illness. Your car might break down, or you could have an accident on the way to the gym. These and other obstacles are hard to manage. We get mad because they put our workout on standby, and when we can't hold it anymore and go there, we work hard for the lost time—and cause injury, making matters worse. And so, when the intruders hit you, it's better to stay home with firm determination to start over when you recuperate. The lack of commitment is as bad. It makes you go only when you feel like going and work hard when you feel powerful and invincible. Chances are, you will work too hard and go home with an injury.

Time off: Whatever the reasons for your planned time off, like vacation, go easy when you restart. Your muscles get weak during the two weeks of vacation, but your brain may not notice the change. You will think you can do what you did two weeks ago—it was easy—but your muscles will let you down, and that will result in injuries.

First and last reps: These can cause injury—beware.

Back support and safety pins: Many gyms provide belts for low-back support. To ensure the use of it whenever you need it, buy your own. Use it every time you squat heavy, bench press, or dead lift heavy, or whenever you feel the need to support your lower back. Don't use it all the time, because you will stop your lower back from getting strong through exercise. Also, strengthen your lower back with low-back and abs exercises; working out your abs makes your back strong. Low-back injury is the worst one to have. It reduces so much of your mobility. Once you mess up your spine, chances are that your life will be badly messed up forever. So use your head and resources available to protect your back—at the gym or outside the gym. The safety pins are recommended for beginners, but I think we should all use them, as they increase the safety for everybody.

Watch out for the days that you feel like a million dollars. There are the days that you feel like you can lift any weights and perform anything. Those are usually the days that stupidity takes over. You push yourself beyond your limits, and injury strikes and laughs at you as you swear and complain of pain, usually shoulders first.

Lift what you can, not what you want. Lift within your strength and endurance. Pushing it beyond your limits will over-stress your muscles and bone, which could cause lifetime injuries. By the way, make sure your partner or spotter gives you that light spot before is too late.

Shoulders: Shoulder injuries happen naturally as we age. It doesn't have to be gym-related. Think about it: we use our shoulders whether standing still, sitting, or lying down. We are creatures on the move, and we make things. Without shoulders, we defeat the human's purpose. When you go to the gym, you increase your shoulders' workload. We go there to improve our health and fitness, and we have gym-related problems only when we do things we were not supposed to do.

When you get hit with shoulder injuries, see your doctor or therapist, or at least work out light and carefully. If the injury gets worse, stop, give it time to heal, and help it with light shoulder exercises and home remedies.

Shoulder injuries vary from mild to severe in many different ways. Surgery and cortisone shots help but only in some cases does the pain go away forever. So the best remedy after a doctor's visit is asking others what has worked for them. Eventually, you will meet someone who had the same injury and will tell you what worked. Here are preventive measures for shoulder injuries:

- Warm up your shoulders before starting any exercise.
- Use light or no weights on the machine to prepare your shoulders for what's coming next. Say you are going to bench press. Use the bar without weights, do five reps, and then begin your routine.
- Watch out for the last rep on heavy bench press. If you can't do it safely, don't do it at all or have your spotter ready.
- Use an experienced spotter.

When you work out your shoulders, keep in mind that you are working a sensitive and very important medium muscle group. Use light weights on most standing exercises, especially dumbbell flies. Here, you are playing with double fire: your shoulders and low back.

Whenever you can, do aerobic exercises for your shoulders. That's one way to take care of small muscles; they support the large muscles you use on heavy lifting.

Push-ups are the number-one physical contest among guys. It's easy to drop to the ground and start doing push-ups. You can win a competition without injuring your shoulders, but it is guaranteed that if you put too much stress on your shoulders, it could cost you later. The older you are, the greater the chances of shoulder injuries on nonstop push-ups. I still play this dangerous game but only on mixed combination with breaks. I love my shoulders; I hate pain.

Get a partner: Lifting heavy all the time demands that you have a spotter. And the best spotter in the world is your partner, but matching schedules is very hard. When your partner can't make it, don't break the routine, but don't be a hero either. Work as hard as when your partner is there with you. Use the weights you can lift by yourself and save the day.

Your Partner and You

We are created identical but not the same; we are unique. Physical appearance seems to be one of the most distinctive human qualities. No matter how identical people are, the strength, endurance, and comfort of performing any physical activities depend on uniqueness, nutrition, and lifestyle of each particular person. Don't try to compete with your partner. Chances are, you will get injuries and lose the partner. Keep in mind that your partner is your friend, spotter, motivator, and lifesaver, not your contender. You can try your partner's strategy, techniques, and machine choices for the purpose of maximizing results and the safety of both of you, but not to prove to him that you can do what he can do. Stick with a program that works for both of you, and save the partnership.

My partner and I are physically opposite. He is bulky from head to toe. I am cut up from head to toe. Our program is high intensity. We use the same machines and exercise almost all the time. Here is how: first, we decide which machines to use for each body part. Usually we select the popular ones; we try them out to see if they could work for us, and then we move to our favorites to finalize our selection. We decide how many weeks for each program; some are six to ten weeks, and others are up to twelve weeks, arbitrarily.

When the selection is not unanimous, I let my partner go with his choices, and on the next program, I go with my choices. We use the same set of weights but different reps. Bench press is an exception, because it happens to be my weakest link and my partner's strongest link. Shoulders are the opposite of that reality, but my partner matches me well.

When we finish one program, we keep the machines and exercises that brought the best results, and if necessary, we make changes to the next program. We used that strategy all the time and did not need to change a thing, because we reached outstanding results. After two years of dedication, motivation, and perseverance, we became the inspiration to friends and gym mates. Our discipline, commitment, and determination were such that people thought we were brothers—actually we were better than brothers. We were the stars!

There you have it: the proof that harmony can rule and great achievement can be reached, despite individual uniqueness, when a good strategy is put to work, and players don't act stupid.

Choosing the Right Partner

You don't have to accept just anyone as a partner. You can say no thanks. If your partner is ignorant, he could give you lifelong injuries. My partner started going to the gym with his longtime friend, who had been a regular at the gym for many years and had achieved outstanding results, even though he lifts to impress, which gives him shoulder injuries all the time.

On the first day, they worked out legs. My partner was matching his friend on heavy squatting. Obviously, he was squatting too much weight; his legs gave up on him. Fortunately, his friend/partner/trainer was near, held the weights, and stopped the disaster from striking on the first set. After this incident, they both became more careful, but he kept matching his friend's lifting techniques. Fortunately, their schedule, strategy, and principles did not work for long. My partner went solo until someone else—better in some ways, worse in other ways—came along. The better was the safety; the worse was the discipline and determination.

Often, they made it to the gym only to decide to work out another day.

Other times, they did not finish the workout, just because the motivation wasn't there. The new partner was not as dangerous as the previous one, but partnering with him was useless. My partner got rid of him; then luck struck, and I came along, proving that choosing a partner is a sensitive issue.

Choosing the right partner requires careful selection to obtain and put to work the necessary partnership principles. Otherwise, the partnership goes nowhere. Commitment and perseverance must be on top of the priority list to ensure success and to progress in the partnership. Some partnerships, depending on the size and nature, require expert consultation and signature of agreements with legal representation. A workout partner doesn't need to go to that extent, but the basic aspects of all partnerships—commitment and perseverance, among other things—must rule. Let's look into some compromises for a workout partner:

- *Commitment*: Commitment must start with you. You must be there and be on time as you agreed, not when you feel like going.
- *Discipline*: This also must start with you. Respect the schedule, and do not be one of the jerks in the gym. If you are, work on you social manners, in the gym and everywhere else. Rack the weights after you use them, and be polite and considerate to others, especially your partner.
- *Perseverance*: If you manage to go to the gym when it's windy, rainy, or snowy, your perseverance is better than many gym-goers.
- *Safety*: Safety must be a top priority. Stay away from anyone who doesn't follow this principle.

After you understand all that, approach those who seem to meet your requirements and discuss the possibility of partnership.

Workout Benefits

When you are fit, your cardiovascular system is fine, your organs of reproduction are fully operational, and your self-esteem is high. You are capable of performing any physical task; employers will see that you can handle physical demands. The opposite sex admires you. Your smile is dazzling and people feel happy around you. You feel the happiness in a way it is supposed to be, plus you will experience the following:

- *Stress reduction.* When you feel stressed out, you hit the gym for one hour or longer. You work out on the treadmill for a half hour, move to the weight section, and work out for another half hour or until you feel tired. You will return home like a feather, and probably with a smile on your face. You could even ask someone to go for a walk.
- *Energy.* Working out gives you an energetic feeling that embraces you everywhere you go, with everything you do, gives the power to go on forever on physical activities, and boosts your self-esteem.
- *Good night's sleep.* Every night, you sleep like a baby.
- *Greater sexual drive.* You don't lie to your soul mate and pretend that you're tired or have a headache.
- *Health.* There is no substitute for exercise and working out on a regular basis.

Veteran

After years of discipline, dedication, motivation, and hard work at the gym, I think you should consider yourself a gym veteran. You earned it. With that title comes a few good things:

- You have reached the workout elite.
- You have learned the language of your muscles.
- You have dominated the laziness and complaints for not going.
- You have enough knowledge and experience to avoid injuries.
- You have the license to work smarter, not harder. You work right, you feel it when you do, and you make programs better than what was given to you. You are never unsure about any machine or type of exercise, and you know right away if they work for you, and

best of all, you no longer have to work so hard to grow; you just work easily to maintain.

Tips

The following tips should be helpful for people engaged in a fitness program at fitness clubs and home gyms:

- *Energy*: Avoid working out on an empty stomach. Have a light meal or snack thirty minutes before your workout, or a full meal two hours before your workout. Protein shakes serve you well here as a quick energy generator. Have a glass before you leave home. Some people drink protein shakes while they work out. Find out what works for you.
- *Water*: Stay hydrated. The harder your workout, the greater the amount of liquid you need to replace. If you dehydrate and continue working out hard, you could faint or even die. So drink water while you're working out but not a gallon at a time. If you drink too much water, you won't work out at your best.
- *Give time the time*: Human nature and social values make us want to get everything now. Don't fall for that, especially in lifting. Relax and enjoy the ride. Unless you jack yourself with steroids and human growth hormones, it will take two to four years of disciplined workout with balanced nutrition for you to get the ultimate lifting results.
- *Lifting power*: Start within your limit and increase the weights by small pounds. I was once told that if I increased two pounds each week, at the end one year, I would increase my total by 104 pounds. Interesting! Of course, you could max out before increasing all that, but the beauty of this principle is that you can start small and grow big in the right way—which, by the way, will not give you injuries.
- *Lift for yourself, not for your partner or anybody in the gym*: It doesn't matter how fit you are; there will always be someone better or

worse than you. The ones looking better than you don't minimize your chances, and the ones looking worse than you don't increase your odds. Focus on getting the best out of you, by doing your thing right and being patient. Soon enough, you will see the results of working out right.

- *Supplement*: Protein is like sex: you have to have it. It will not only fuel your muscle but also will help you to better your health and fitness due to its composition, including vitamins and minerals that otherwise you couldn't have. But don't abuse it—too much of a good thing is bad for you. Also, get as much information as possible to help you choose the right protein for you. There are so many brands on the market, but not all the brands are good for you. It never hurts to ask your doctor's opinion on adding protein or any other supplement to your diet. Because protein shakes change bowel movement in some people, give some time for your body to adjust. Change the brand if weeks go by and your body can't adjust.

- *Rest*: It is not a crime to work out at the gym every day, but I don't think it would be a wise move. I have friends who go to the gym every day. I understand that they don't work out crazy, and they probably spend most of their time in the gym doing cardio, but I still think that's crazy. You must give your body what it needs to rejuvenate—rest. And if you work out to gain muscle, you must rest your muscles or see slow gain.

- *Surprise your muscles*: One of the secrets to maximizing your workout results is muscle surprise. Almost all the gym-goers tell you that. That's why gyms have a variety of machines designed to target the same body part. Keep an eye open to spot people doing something new and interesting. Try it out on your next program. If it works for you, keep it; if it doesn't, forget it, and find your own new machine and exercise.

- *Time*: Eliminate distractions and time-consuming actions such as phone calls and long conversations. Keep in mind that the gym is not a chat or gossip room.

- *Be wise and broaden your knowledge*: Read magazines, ask friends and experts, or go online to search about health and fitness. There is a wealth of information online. Just use common sense to distinguish truthful from bogus information.

- *Total workout*: As you begin weight lifting, realize that you must work out your entire body. Work your abs, neck, back, shoulders, arms (biceps, triceps, forearms, and wrists), and legs, including calves. You can divide your muscle groups as large and small or large, medium, and small. Chest, back, and legs are large; leg muscles are the largest.

Most people consider all the other muscle groups (shoulders, biceps, triceps, calves, and neck) as small groups, but others divide them into medium and small groups. I don't think specifics matter here, but if you need to know, you can search online or ask a doctor or physical therapist. What matters the most is that you work all your muscles.

Don't think you should give priority to your chest because that's what you use to show off your muscles and forget about legs because they are covered by your pants. Your legs are the foundation of your body, a huge reason to keep them in top shape.

Give attention to small muscles so you can get better support for your physical activities, fewer chances for injuries in and out of gym, and health and fitness benefits from head to toe.

Don't work out just to look good on your next summer vacation. You should work out for the health and fitness benefits throughout the year, for as long as you live.

Health and fitness—the topic is almost endless. Fitness brings the best health out in you, and to get the best fitness out of you, you need to exercise and lift weights. Let's throw away excuses and join fitness clubs, get a home gym, or use both to live a better, longer, healthier life, starting right now.

16

Nutrition

It's AMAZING HOW DESTRUCTIVE WE human beings are. Everything we lay our hands on ends up broken or destroyed. It's the consequence of crazy, curious behavior or stubbornness, pushing us to find the next better thing than what we have in hand. Have you ever watched your kids examining toys? No matter how many things the toys can do, they look for something new, better, and different from the toys they have. If better is what comes next, soon they find themselves looking for the best, better than the best, and better than that. It never stops. Breaking things to fix creates something new and different, and that makes our lives easier and better most of the time and difficult some of the time. Since the discovery of fire, we have been walking this trend of breaking to fix and creating new and different things in all aspects of life. So why should nutrition, as important as it is, be an exception to the rule?

I believe that the Lord provides natural nutrition in a wide variety of colors, shapes, and tastes so no one will go hungry—fruits, meat, and drinking water from land, and fish from oceans, rivers, and ponds are all ready for us. I don't understand why the Lord provided nutrition that will kill us; I guess that's part of the big mystery, but we learn ways to select what to eat for survival and stay away from poisonous ones.

Fire revolutionized our living processes, bringing us to light from darkness, but it also touched the culinary area. Restaurants serve the most delicious meals to please our taste buds, accompanied by their own specialties. We love food so much that we created culinary schools! Then technology gave us refrigeration to conserve frozen food and save leftovers, microwaves to heat up and cook meals supersonically, and on and on. The food industry supplies food through fast-food restaurants and vending machines. We created hundreds of food supplements in many varieties—dry food, pills, just add water and microwave it, protein shakes and so on. The abundance and revolution of food are such that there is no excuse for people to suffer malnutrition, especially in this country.

In reality, however, millions of people suffer from hunger. Children go to bed on empty stomachs in this country and around world. Restaurants and military kitchens in rich countries dump leftovers in the garbage, while hunger kills every day and everywhere.

The Food and Drug Administration (FDA) has done a good job of guarding us from harm, but it can't find ways to fix the problem of wasted food that could feed the hungry. Don't get me wrong—there are many organizations and agencies, private and governmental, aiming to rid the country and the world of starvation, but it seems that lots of things are not working right in this aspect. And until this problem is resolved, we have to bear the shame, and this is on top of another big problem—excess weight and obesity.

Do You Have What It Takes?

This is a touchy issue, but I hope to shed some light on the problem of overweight and obesity. Still, some people don't like to acknowledge the problem. Consider this example: a few years ago, my neighbor Jennifer, who had been taking martial arts classes, had a chubby high school friend over to visit. I gave them rides a few times to their friend's house in town, and we became sort of friends. One day the conversation was about karate. Jennifer's friend said that she wished she could take classes too. I encouraged her to do so for a variety of reasons. They both agreed with me—until I mentioned that karate would help Jennifer's friend lose some weight.

The silence that immediately followed proved that I had hit a wrong note. Finally, Jennifer broke the silence, saying, "Don't you know that you should never call a girl fat?"

"I did not call her fat," I said, trying to defend myself.

"Yeah, you did," Jennifer insisted.

"I told her that karate would help her lose some—"

"That's the same thing, Arlindo!" Jennifer cut short my attempt to explain. I was outnumbered, so why continue the fight, right? Besides, the silence of Jennifer's friend made me feel guilty. I also knew right then that after I dropped them off, the conversation would emerge again. I hoped Jennifer would tell me about it the next day. She did.

"Do you know that you made my friend cry yesterday?" Jennifer asked. "Well, she didn't cry, but she called you an asshole."

"Jennifer, I was being honest in a nice way, and you know that," I said defensively but without hostility.

"Arlindo, it doesn't matter! You can never call a girl fat—never," she said seriously.

As you see, it's a sensitive topic, but we must not let excess weight and obesity go in peace. They are taking too many of us and too much money with them. And so, let's stand strong to talk about them and point out some quick fixes. But first, let's define the terms. The World Health Organization defines *obesity* as abnormal or excessive fat accumulation that may impair health. The body mass index (BMI) is a measurement that compares weight to height and is used to classify excess weight and obesity in adults. A person with a BMI between twenty-five and thirty is overweight; a BMI greater than thirty indicates obesity.

Our active genes, which define who we are now and will be later, were inherited from our ancestors, who inherited them from their ancestors on an infinite spiral. The sperm marathon to fertilize our mother's egg gives all the prizes to one winner. Millions of contenders were released when our father dynamited during sex with our mother, but only one contender wins that single prize. On that three- to five-day marathon, so many low-hanging fruits will be collected en route to shape our faces, similar to taking a filthy car to the car wash—you pay for the service, put your car in neutral, and the conveyor takes it through the washing process. Different kinds of soaps and washing detergents will be dumped and sprayed on the car before it reaches the high-power clear-water washing and finally to high-power air blowers. The soaps and detergents will trigger the changes on your car in time to come. The washing could contribute to paint discoloration and rust on the car years from now. You may get rid of the car before the changes become noticeable, but the ingredients to trigger the changes are there. This is analogous to being a victim of ancestry.

If your obesity is not due to lack of exercise or being deeply in love with burgers, chips, pizza, sausages, and others among food's weapons of "massive destruction," then somewhere down on the sperm marathon road, some of your ancestors sprayed fat genes on you and on all your brothers and sisters, but you happened to be the weakest link, and those fat genes are making your body a nightclub dance floor, and the boogie is on. But aside from the tragedy, you are still in charge of this party. It's your party. You can control it by kicking out those who are causing the most noise. If you don't do anything, however, the boogie will go on—you'll become obese.

If you suffer from obesity, the fault might be your own. Food's weapons of massive destruction are your best friends; you take them everywhere with you, and go everywhere with them! What the hell are you doing? You are taking this festival to places you've never gone before in a chaotic way. Look at yourself! What a disgrace! Can you imagine how much worse this obesity festival would be if your fat genes start acting up? Still, you can get your act together and restore order to this fat festival. Obesity is not your best friend. It is your worst enemy.

Some people don't know how they became obese. In this case, controlling the fat boogie is more challenging. It doesn't mean that you should cross your arms and hope to die. It just means that the work to restore order in the obesity house party is harder and could take longer.

Which Way?

Whatever is the cause of obesity, the big controversy about accepting or fighting obesity still stands. It seems there are many overweight and obese people undecided about whether to fight or accept their condition, due to lack of an appropriate incentive and clear information, among other issues.

Even though many of us look like fat gorillas, I don't think that's how we started out. If we did, at sometime and somewhere along the millions of years of human evolution, we developed slim genes, and we put them to work for obvious reasons. It's evident that on becoming loose creatures on the move, constantly discovering, creating, and innovating things to meet living demands, the slimmer we were, the better our chances of survival and accomplishment. Then, the genes responsible for passion, love, and attraction drove us to be slim, sexy, and beautiful. Genes of bias, choice, selection, and so on kicked in too. Here we are in the age of the technology explosion and media dominance, where rich and sexy rule. The media, paparazzi, and government dictate today how we should live and change all that the next day. The urgency to measure up and raise the bars—with money, sex, drugs, and alcohol—is the real reality of today's world, leaving overweight and obese people behind. Maybe now more than in years past, being overweight spells big trouble and being obese is a death warrant. But that is not the reason why we should fight excess weight and obesity. It doesn't matter how hard media, paparazzi, and the government try to control our lives; we will always be in charge. The final say belongs to us. Overweight, obese, or slim, our values, integrity, and philosophical principles are untouchable until we say otherwise.

On the other side of the coin, we may find that being overweight or obese is part of what we are, because our genetics allow it to be.

Fat Is What We Are

There are hundreds of reasons why we should take care of ourselves to the best of our abilities. That means health and fitness before anything else. Being healthy and fit is not spelled overweight and obese by any means, but there are those who think that if our genetics allow us to become overweight and obese, then that is what we are. In some cultures, being overweight is an indication of well-being. Kids are considered in good hands if they are chubby; otherwise, they'd be starving and probably carrying some illness or disease. A married woman who's slim and sexy is thought of as suffering stress and depression from marriage or starving to death.

It is true that our genetics define who we are and will be—short or tall, slim or fat, healthy or sickly. If we are genetically fat, it pretty much comes down to finding ways to mold the world in a way that we can live being overweight or obese, happily forever after. We cross our arms and hope to die overweight or obese … except that things are not quite that simple. Taking into consideration the fight for survival in the world, should we or should we not accept what we are: freaks of fat?

By accepting what we are, we will need to introduce drastic changes, individually and worldwide, in the way we eat, dress, travel, and interact. Let's begin with food and beverages. To be like King Kong, we need to eat and drink like King Kong, worsening the world's starvation. Remember, numerous factors are responsible for the world's starvation, but the main problem here is supply. Food supply has not been able to follow population growth. As we pack on more pounds, we see an extension of our waist, stomach bloating, and the need to increase clothing sizes (meaning greater amounts of fabric to clothe each of us). Our apartments, houses, or shelter will expand to fit our larger furniture—couples will need a king-sized bed. Public facilities will need to be bigger to accommodate the large creatures that we will become. Compact cars will get the kiss of death, while the airplanes will take the biggest blow.

It's not discrimination against gender, color, ethnicity, or appearance that makes airlines ask passengers for information about their weight before assigning seats to them. It's the weight-and-balance issue. First of all, inside an airplane, overweight and obese people get center seats, and the slimmer passengers sit near the windows, so the airplane will not tip to one side, up or down. It must be balanced, or the flight will be doomed.

Second, a plane full of light passengers will fly easier and faster, and that saves fuel. Third, if you have flown, you might have noticed how difficult it is for overweight and obese people to fit in those airplane seats. The industry wouldn't like to have larger seats, because doing so reduces the number of seats on an airplane. Fourth, an airplane can carry only so much weight, or it won't leave the ground. When overweight and obese people take most of the specific weight allowance, just a few pounds of carry-ons and luggage will be allowed. If this has been a problem, imagine how bad it will become.

As we keep moving on in the aeronautic industry, we get to space adventure. We are about to start private trips to space and to colonize other planets. I am not sure that overweight and obese people will be allowed to go, no matter how much money they have.

Militarily speaking, we will be safer than ever, as the only way to fight will be sitting on our fat asses in the office. Drones come in handy. Dogfights are about to disappear, as long-range air-to-air missiles will take over and later be replaced by lasers and other weaponry. But even then, we will still need pilots in fighter jets for close and personal businesses. Can you see overweight and obese people qualifying for that kind of mission? Good-bye army, navy SEAL, and all sorts of fighting that requires bodies on the move.

The Income World

To be like King Kong, we need to eat and drink like King Kong, but where will we get the extra cash for extra food? We will physically be unable to work more than one full-time job. You see, being obese harms our chances of getting a good-paying job. If you still manage to keep your job, a chunk of your check will go to health care. Chances are, we will rely on free care to cover our health costs for the health problems that we created by ourselves for ourselves. We have thousands of veterans coming home with post-traumatic stress disorder, injured, and disabled, all in need of government support. Their urgent help starts with health care. Obesity's free care is taking funds that should go to these warriors who fought for you to keep your right to life, liberty, and the pursuit of happiness. Think about it—you are making yourself sick and demanding to be taken care of, while those who legitimately need care will not get it because you keep taking pieces of the pie that are not yours. And how will we fight the double challenge: extra food and the cash for extra food?

Sports World

Sports are almost as important as the air we breathe. Worldwide, now more than ever, sports are great money generators. Players get tons of it, coaches get tons of it, and even lucky fans get some of it. Owners, unions, and the government all get some of it. I think we place sports next to national security, health care, global warming, and world conventions, if not ahead of them.

What sports can we keep when we embrace being overweight and obese as a way of life? Here are some that definitely will be gone:

- running
- tennis
- basketball
- baseball
- volleyball
- football
- soccer
- ice skating
- cycling
- gymnastics

Hell, No!

With the science of medicine lagging behind diseases since day one, we have reached the critical stage, where we desperately need doctors to make miracles and cure diseases. Giving them license to be overweight and obese will not solve our obesity problems; it will bring more problems and make them more complicated. Will the health staff be able to take care of their overweight and obese patients when they are more overweight than their patients? Probably not—but who cares? Because we are all fat, we will adjust to the new us, the freaks of fat, and live forever happy, right? Not so fast, buddy! We have bigger fish to fry, some not even caught yet: national security defense; war on terrorism; drug wars; wars brought to us and taken to others; cyber wars; fights for verification that those claiming to be allies are real friends, not foes; spies in the skies, oceans, and lands; tornadoes, hurricanes, floods, earthquakes, and tsunamis; global warming; ocean pollution; deforestation; species extinction; flu viruses and pandemic fears; fears of nuclear attacks, alien invasion and meteorite crashes; fears of Communism; inflation; job losses, international crises; welfare; international aid and aid to search and research; world starvation; homelessness; immigration; border security; Social Security; health care; and secret projects, all forming one long line of major issues.

Let me remind you that money doesn't grow on trees. So I don't think the government will allow us to be as fat as we wish, even if we compromise and pay very high taxes for it. But let's assume the world has decided to embrace global obesity. As soon as we open the gates of super-size and "be as overweight as you wish," we will face riots from slim people and lawsuits from the civil rights movement, as not everybody will want to be obese and deal with the hassle from it. It will come to Democrats on one side and Republicans on the other, both trying to do it right, but both getting it wrong and worsened each time they try.

The government will not take away the right that people have to choose a lifestyle, but it has the right to make sure that everybody has a lifestyle that will not conflict with the lifestyle of others. For instance, the funds to cure illnesses from obesity will not cover the needs, but the government will not increase it because funds for other illnesses and diseases will be hurt.

It is almost impossible for overweight and obese people to keep up with the fast pace of a lifestyle that's becoming demanding. Does it seem realistic to embrace global obesity? Of course not! It is, in many ways, clear that being slim is the best choice for human survival.

Our philosophical principles and differences in beliefs don't change the state of the matter. They can only influence our observation, power of analysis, and behavior. So regardless of what we believe and stand for, you and I arrive at the same chaotic Main Street, where health, nutrition, obesity, and starvation are fighting a complicated war. The single common mission is for all of us to give our best contribution to this Main Street, so it can find peace and harmony. We might have to introduce changes in our nutritional style and mold our attitude toward a more conservative approach, so we can help ourselves and each other win the war on all fronts.

On one front we face the bombardment of food availability and advertisements focused on keeping us locked so we can eat more than what we need, sucking our dollars and reducing the chances of others to get proper nutrition. We are chained down by the food industry. If Burger King and McDonald's were to serve free meals, they would make sandwiches so distasteful that people would never come back. Fast-food restaurants and regular restaurants make our visits pleasant by serving us delicious food, so we will come back and bring our friends.

Fast food and processed food are the worst to consume, and we know it, but this type of food is least expensive and available to us everywhere, so it becomes an irresistible temptation. No one is pointing a gun to our heads to eat junk food or drink soda. As a matter of fact, that bag of potato chips, candy bar, and can of soda come in handy sometimes. So the secret to eating junk food and sweet beverages without harming yourself lies in you: consume them within your tolerance. Your friends can eat many cheeseburgers, Big Macs, bologna sandwiches, and cheese pizzas every week without getting fat or seeing their cholesterol level go up. Their metabolism is that good. If yours is not that good, watch your fat intake.

The real fight is happening on other fronts. That is where we fight all kinds of problems generated by the first front. The FDA still requires the food industry to display nutrition facts on food packages and containers to give us the opportunity to know what we are eating. There are hotlines to call to report food poisonings, recalls of contaminated food, and on and on, aiming toward nutrition safety and the well-being of everybody. The government wants us to spend as much money as we can on good food, so we can stay healthy, go to work, and make a lot of money, so it can collect more taxes from us. It also does not want us to get fat, especially when we don't pay for our own health insurance. But with all this power, knowledge, and awareness, we are still not catching up to obesity. We are losing, and the game can't go on like this. The following considerations should wake us up to fight excess weight and obesity:

Society: When an overweight person walks by, we can't keep bias and prejudice from acting up. That's a strong, natural, bad behavior we've inherited. Some of us may deny it, but we all know it will always be there. Many slim people believe that overweight and obese people stand in the way of their own success and the success of others. Others think that overweight and obese people are lazy and disgusting, and they themselves are to blame for being overweight or obese.

We happen to be social human beings. Even though we have the right to speak our personal opinions, observations, and peculiarities, as social human beings we have to respect the social values imposed on us. Society expects us to make appropriate adjustments to our private world, when necessary, so we comply for our sanity and the sanity of others. Prejudice or bias against being overweight doesn't help, and being obese makes it almost impossible to comply with social demands. Excessive fat brings a variety of health problems.

Victims of genetics deserve sympathy for the flaws of their genes. Still, they should do what they can to make sure that excess weight and obesity don't take away their right to life, liberty, and the pursuit of happiness. They have to make a little bit more of a sacrifice than slim people do but shouldn't feel bad or discouraged; this is life—unfair.

Now let me tell you about your wardrobe and character. The way you present yourself says a lot about you. Don't wear tight clothing. It will shape fat bumps all over your body, especially your upper body. Use loose-fitting, light fabric—silk wouldn't be a bad choice. Women, whenever you can, wear a dress or skirt and blouse instead of jeans and a sweater. When you dress recklessly, you look despicable. If you have an angry face and rude manners to go with it, you will make matters worse. You can be sure that people will call you a fat bitch when you walk away. To avoid tragedies or creating more enemies, dress in fresh clothing, make sure you feel pretty, and keep a smile on your face with a friendly attitude everywhere you go. That smile is a sign of happiness. You were born beautiful, but you must maintain your natural beauty with makeup, clothing, attitude, and education. Even if you are overweight or obese, no one can stop you from bringing out the beauty in you. When you feel like a million dollars, others will look at you as two million dollars. This approach should be taken by everyone. Check with fashion designers and follow suggestions in fashion magazines. Don't let anybody tell you that you can't be pretty and likable because you are overweight or obese. Just remember, though, that diet and exercise brings greater beauty out of you.

To overweight guys, it doesn't matter how fancy your wardrobe is. It won't change much of your situation. That doesn't mean, though, that you should neglect your looks and hygiene. Everything gets worse with excess weight and obesity.

Negative psychological effects: Some people create a great deal of stress for overweight and obese people through nice gestures such as holding the doors, helping to carry grocery bags, giving up seats on busses, and so on. These gestures make them feel incapable of taking care of themselves. Even though they welcome the gestures most of the time and do not feel inferior, the negative psychological effects is either invisibly or visibly there. On the other hand, there are times when help would be appreciated, but there wouldn't be any, because people don't know if their help would be accepted. The negative psychological effect in this case is immediately noticeable, because the person will ask for help with a demanding attitude or mumble about people's rudeness. Either way, these scenarios cause negative psychological effect on those who are overweight or obese.

Crowded market: We don't seem to be able to control our birthrate. We just reached a world population of seven billion people. We spit out more girls than boys. Boys get killed in wars and in stupid stunts such as car racing, gang shootouts, and so forth, tipping the already uneven balance of gender even further. Being handsome and financially secure are required of men to earn a sex partner. The challenge is more difficult if you are overweight or obese.

Sex: This should catch our attention for many reasons: sexual ecstasy, given to us by the Creator or the big bang is the most rewarding thing yet to human beings, and I think it extends to all living creatures. Since our childhood, we have been attracted to slim, sexy, and beautiful first and then to the rest. Slim and beautiful people wake up our passion and sexual desires instantly and keep the windows open for love at first sight. The overweight and obese ones don't carry those extraordinary powers. We mock them—sometimes to their faces, more often behind their backs—we call them names and rarely pick them to play on our team unless we overcome bias and stupidity, accept them as what they are, and make them our beautiful overweight friends. Even so, the more overweight you are, the greater the chances of being left for last. Notice that I said left for last, not saved for last, because you are not the best.

This trend of attraction grows with us. Society condones it, and the media measures it with hypocrisy in such a way that those who are slim, sexy, and beautiful appear to be the only ones to carry sexual powers. In reality, you can find slim and sexy people who suck in bed as well as obese people who surprise you with action. But sex is way too important for us not to care about it.

To begin with, sex is the ultimate reason we seek relationships. When we are dating without plans for commitment, it keeps us in touch before anything else. The greater the sex is, the stronger the connection; the poorer the sex, the greater the chances of breaking up. And when we commit, sex takes an even higher position because now, it serves many more purposes than just pleasure, such as the main source of stress relief. When you are obese, there is no denying that your actions are poor. If your actions are poor, your sexual activities are poor. Besides, poor sex leads to relationship malfunctions, from cheating to divorce.

Obesity can be murder in sex too. I clearly remember that some skinny guy had sex with an obese girl. She fell asleep on top of him. They were both drunk. The girl woke up; the guy didn't.

Sexual taboos and biases have been passed on to us and will be passed on to future generations with a few more flavors and choices from each generation's exploration and discoveries, in combination with genes of love, passion, and pleasure. Sexy and beautiful take the best prizes. Any extra pound standing in the way will always minimize the chances of sexual enjoyment at a full potential. That is such a tragedy!

Employment: Even in a good economy, employers think that productivity of overweight and obese employees could be higher if they were slim and fit. For that, the opportunity for raises and promotions could be delayed for them. They could be the first ones to be laid off and the last ones to be called back. They get regular raises and promotions because the employers are making good money off them, and there is a backup plan in case they have to take a long time off to take care of health complications from excess weight and obesity, such as high blood pressure, stroke, or heart attack.

At the end of 2012, the world's economy was still struggling to stay above the water, never mind standing on firm, dry land, which we all need desperately. Those who are employed fear layoffs or bankruptcy, which has been sweeping the world, as well as the pressure to meet performance standards, which is increased every now and then and monitored like a hawk. Any employee constantly below standards will receive warnings about performance. Fast-paced is pretty much the name of the game; you have to stay on your toes to keep up and stay employed. You don't have many chances to catch a breath or two, because people are waiting in a long line for your job. As an overweight or obese employee, how do you stand a chance to keep your job?

Those who are unemployed feel the frustration of not finding places that are hiring or of being turned down for being under- or over-qualified. To make matters worse, the longer you stay unemployed, the greater the chances of your not being qualified, as many places hiring don't accept applicants who have been unemployed for more than six months. The screening of applicants is more detailed, because the numbers are overwhelming. Places like warehouses, where lifting is required, submit applicants to a surprise lifting test. Unsafe lifting gives you a red mark on your application.

If you are overweight or obese, besides presumptions of being less productive, you are telling the hiring staff that you will call in sick more often than your coworkers and that the chances of liability on you are higher than the applicants who are healthy and fit. Chances are, you will be scratched off the list. Do those who are overweight or obese stand a good chance to find a job? I don't think so!

Health: This is also an obesity issue. Our internal organs are working twenty-four/seven so we can stay the way we were meant to stay: lean and active. Under normal conditions, we grow proportionally as the rest of living creatures. Maybe we started out differently, but this is how we ended up. We don't see people with gigantic heads and tiny bodies unless there has been a birth deformity. Under normal conditions, an individual over age twenty-five doesn't grow anymore. He can only expand. An expansion of size doesn't mean the enlargement of internal organs. If it does, you can be sure that's not a good thing. At that age, an individual standing five foot eight, at 140 or 150 pounds, with a thirty-two-inch waist is within an acceptable height/weight range. Increasing your weight to three hundred pounds will not increase the size of your heart, lungs, liver, or kidneys. It will increase the workload of your heart, liver, kidneys, and your lungs, which are the hardest-working organs in your body, supplying oxygen to your tissues and expelling carbon dioxide from your body. If you are overweight, they must work harder to reach every corner of your enlargement to keep you alive and well.

House chores: Assuming that you can afford a maid, you still need to do your part, at least on the weekends. I am sure there will be some cooking, washing, cleaning, and a hundred other little things that seem easy to do but are tiring. Taking care of the kids doubles or triples your house chores, causing you to leave a lot of things for next week or for the maid. I just don't know how long your maid will stay working for you when your obesity prevents you from doing your chores.

Emergency rescue: Each day we hear of situations that made people run for their lives, such as natural disaster, accidents, and human brutality. It makes it harder for the rescue team to take people to safety if they are overweight or obese. It doesn't matter where we are; there is no safety for any of us these days, which makes it even more important that we stay healthy, slim, and fit to escape deadly dangers that require running for our lives.

Entertainment: The more diversified your entertainment world is, the greater is your body/mind/spirit balance. Say you go to the movies, clubs, parties, church, public events, concerts, or on walks to the beach and parks. You play with your friends, your kids, your spouse, and you watch comedy at home. All these activities are good for you. Laughter, for example, is like fuel for your health, with comedy bringing out the best in you. Going to a club is the best of the best, assuming that when you go, you only have a few drinks and dance all night long. That's how you get the full benefit. If you are overweight or obese, you can't get the full benefit because, for one, you will be embarrassed to go to clubs. Second, you can't boogie all night, or you will die. So your entertainment will consist of lying down on the couch, with a burger, soda, and fries within arm's reach, to watch comedy and get fatter at the same time.

Health care: All the fights to fix health care are based on cost and maybe a little bit of consideration to the taxpayers. Do you know how much money government has spent on obesity-related illnesses? Do you know how many projects the government could have begun with the money spent on those illnesses? If I had all the resources available for people to monitor their heath, I would tell them that sitting on their fat asses and getting fatter is bad for their health and the health of others. Scientists, doctors, health technicians, and specialists have not given us the green lights to be overweight and obese. Fat complications are numerous and real—high blood pressure, stroke, heart attack, and diabetes are most common. Diabetes is an alarming obesity problem due to the number of patients diagnosed and the number of diabetes-related deaths each year. And now it is attacking children too.

Obesity is a problem itself, and it brings brothers and sisters to help kill us. The time has come to put on the gloves and jump in the ring. Obesity has asked for it; now it's going to get it. The fight will not be Mike Tyson–style, because obesity will impose strong resistance and stand for a long battle, but we have diet and exercise as our coach and assistant coach. We are geared up to take it down. It may not happen on the first, second, or third round, but we are confident that obesity will go down with a knockout punch.

Kids and Nutrition

To you parents, please change the direction of things for your kids. They don't have control over themselves, and that includes what they eat. Their first choice is what tastes sweet and delicious, which is generally unhealthy. Control intake of sugar-filled foods to reduce the risk of diabetes, and control that fat and calorie intake. Give special attention to fast foods to reduce the chances of obesity.

And to you obese kids, products of your fat parents, you don't have to follow this family tradition. You don't have to let your parents or anybody make you any fatter. Take control of your destiny and enjoy life, slim and healthy.

The Plan to Lose Pounds

Speed is now the name of every game. Speed is one of the plagues inherited from the twentieth century. As we live the moment, we just can't escape the traps of speed because they are everywhere we go, even when praying! There's the temptation to skip some words on purpose to get to the end faster. When the priest is taking his time, we feel tempted to shout, "Priest, get on with it! We have places to go and faces to see!" Some things when rushed, however, will just not do well. Diet is one of them. Rush your diet, and count on disappointing results. Smart marketers use this trend of the speedy life we live to fool people with unrealistic diet programs, such as "You can lose twenty pounds in one week. Guaranteed or your money back." Funny thing—we do get fooled. So what you want to do is diet with common sense. Most people give up on their diet and gain back what they lost because they don't diet right. So let's try things differently this time, with just a few steps to consider.

The first step to diet right is determination. Determination will keep you in touch with a way to reach your goals. The second step is patience. The more pounds you need to lose, the longer the time to get there. You know that. You don't need anybody to tell you that. It is obvious that it's unrealistic to lose 150 pounds in three months. You see, losing weight is not something you take a crash course for, or the results will be catastrophic. Your body would not have time to adjust to the drastic changes; it will die on you. So set a number, say one pound per week, and multiply that for the pounds you need to lose. That gives you the time it will take you. This is an easy formula that anybody can do. You lose about fifty-two pounds per year. In three years, you can lose 156 pounds, and keep your life with great health and fitness. Do you even know how fast three years will go by? I just know that four years have passed since you made that New Year's resolution to start a diet and exercise; five years have passed since you kicked that fat, cheating liar out of your life—and it seems like yesterday! If you need to lose three hundred pounds, it will take just six years.

The third step is control. This is as important as steps one and two combined. Control means watching your progress, making adjustments when necessary, and continuing the journey. Things will not work according to plan. You know that from experience. A lot of things will make you go a week or two below your minimum weight loss. You could even gain weight there. If you do, get angry and then get back to the gym tomorrow. Work a bit harder than last week, and cut down just a bit more on your calorie intake. If you are lucky and see clearly why you didn't meet the target, all you need to do is stop doing what you did, and do what you should be doing. Stay always in control of the situation. If you have a setback that's out of your control, restart your program when you can. Prove to yourself that you are in control. Never rely on luck. Keep doing what you are doing and enjoy the results.

The last step is maintenance. When you reach your desired weight, the work doesn't end there. You need to maintain that weight. That could be tricky, because if you stay in your diet program, you will continue to lose. If you drop your diet plan, you will gain. Don't panic and begin to eat like a horse and stop exercise. You will start getting fat again. To avoid the drama, keep a current exercise program or change programs. Nobody's weight stays the same. It varies between five and ten pounds. You decide how many pounds you want above or below your target. Whenever you don't like the numbers, just take care of them. Say you see yourself getting ten pounds above your target. Increase exercise, eat less, and watch the weight go down, or exercise less and eat more to gain what you need to gain.

You don't have to eliminate all your favorite foods from your diet. Just eat them in less quantity and increase the amounts of good food when you need to eat more. Also, if you want to eliminate a dish, this is the best way to do it: have a smaller amount each time. No hassle, no stress, no sickness—just a gradual evaporation.

Calories, one of the main sources of energy for our body, are also the main factor in making us overweight and obese. The body transforms calories from foods and drinks into energy (fuel) for our activities and maintenance. Calories from good sources (good calories) are welcomed and used right away by the body. Any leftover is sent to the recycle bin for future use, if necessary. The problem is that as soon as it gets to the recycle bin, it's transformed into fat. The calories from junk foods (bad calories) are used right away only when you are starving. Otherwise, the body will send the whole thing to the recycle bin. You should consume about 2,500 calories per day. The second source of energy is the carbohydrates, one of the main types of nutrients and the most important source of energy for your body, and you are supposed to have about 350 grams per day. The third source of energy is fat calories. You are supposed to have about 75 grams per day. And from that, anything with more than 3 grams of saturated fat is considered not good. Any leftovers form carbohydrates, and fat is sent to the recycle bin to sit next to bad calories and good calories that are leftovers—and you know what happens there.

When you are on a diet, you need foods low in calories, carbohydrates, and fat. This way, you can eat a big plate or two and still not reach your maximum intake, so there will be a room for ice cream. You can find foods low in calories all over the place. You don't find foods low in carbohydrates and low in fat all over the place. And here comes the killer: when you find good calories, either carbohydrates or fat is high. When you find low carbohydrates, the fat is high. When you find low calories and low fat, the carbohydrates are high. Basically, it's impossible to get enough of the good stuff without too much bad stuff taking a free ride, which calls your attention to the portion of food you will have on your losing-weight program. Let's read the nutrition facts of a couple of items and understand the difference to help us pick the best choice.

One frozen chicken breast sandwich
Serving size: 1 sandwich (122 g)
Serving per container: 1
Calories: 340; calories from fat: 110
Total fat: 12 g (representing 18% of daily value. Daily value is what you are supposed to have per day)
Saturated fat: 1 g (representing 5% of daily value)
Sodium: 710 mg (representing 28% of daily value)
Total carbohydrates: 43 g (representing 14% of daily value)
Cholesterol: 25 mg (representing 8% of daily value)

One hot dog
Serving size: 1 link (1 hot dog) 43 g
Calories: 130; calories from fat: 100
Total fat: 11 g (representing 17% of daily value)
Saturated fat: 3.5 g (representing 17% of daily value)
Sodium: 510 mg (representing 21% of daily value)
Total carbohydrates: 2 g (representing 1% of daily value)
Cholesterol: 30 mg (representing 11% of daily value)

One cheeseburger
Serving size: 1 sandwich (130 g)
Calories: 370; calories from fat: 160
Total fat: 18 g (representing 28% of daily value)
Saturated fat: 8 g (representing 39% of daily value)
Sodium: 620 mg (representing 26% of daily value)
Total carbohydrates: 33 g (representing 11% of daily value)

Cholesterol: 45 mg (representing 15% of daily value)

One bag of potato chips
Serving size: 1 oz (28 g about 12 chips)
Calories: 150; calories from fat: 70
Total fat: 8 g (representing 12% of daily value)
Saturated fat: 1 g (representing 5% of daily value)
Sodium: 180 mg (representing 8% of daily value)
Total carbohydrates: 18 g (representing 6% of daily value)
Cholesterol: 0 mg

Percent daily values are based on 2,000 calories per day. Your daily values may be higher or lower, depending on your calorie needs.

From the choices above, none is a healthy choice. If calories are good, fat and fat calories are not, or if those are good, cholesterol or something else is bad. So it goes with almost all type of foods—you can't win. But you can work your way around it. If you compare all the numbers, you see that you win with chicken, primarily because a hot dog is low in total calories and high in fat calories. (In the chicken sandwich, you have 340 calories, with less than 30 percent in fat calories, while in that hot dog, you have 130 calories and about 80 percent in fat calories.)

You can see that hot dogs and chips are poor choices, because we can easily devour a bag of chips, five hot dogs, and a can of soda and still be hungry an hour later. This means we will have to eat a couple of sandwiches and drink a cup of orange juice to satisfy the hunger. On the other hand, almost any plate of cooked food (rice, beans, corn, potato, spaghetti, meat, fish, vegetable, and so on) will keep you full and keep your body happier for much longer than sandwiches and junk foods. And this takes us to the difference between quantity and quality.

Hot dogs, chips, Twinkies, chocolate bars, and sodas give numerous calories and other nutrients that your body will send to the recycle bin. They are not the nutrients that your body needs for its maintenance (protein, vitamins, minerals). A plate of any meat with a little bit of mashed potato, rice, beans, and carrots are what your body loves and thanks you for.

Almost none of them will go to the recycle bin, and that will reduce the chances of your body looking like a product of Idaho.

Let's clarify things a little bit here: the vitamin C you get from a chocolate bar is not the same as the vitamin C from an orange or a glass of orange juice. Your body wants that from the orange as first choice, and orange juice for a second choice. The same thing happens to the protein of a hot dog, chocolate bar, glass of milk, or an ounce of cereal. Your body prefers the protein from lean meat, chicken breast, or fish. It will use the whole thing or send just a bit of it to the liver for disposal. It's like buying clothes and shoes—you need to wear clothes to protect your skin and because society doesn't allow you to walk naked in public. So you select clothing that you like and that is a good fit. Your shoes are bad, however, if they are too small and hurt your feet, and you give yourself knee pain and maybe lower back pain too.

When your body uses up the energy from good calories and it needs more energy, it restores junk from the recycle bin and turns it back to good calories (energy, fuel), leaving some space in the recycle bin. That's what we call burning extra calories. As long as you keep restoring junk from the recycle bin, you are fine, slim, or losing weight. When you don't burn calories and keep eating like King Kong, the leftovers from good calories, bad calories, carbohydrates, and fats will all go to the recycle bin. When the place gets too crowded, the recycle bin will tell the guests to take a hike. They leave to find a new home in your belly. That's why you keep getting fat. That's why it is recommended that you burn more calories than what you take in, or keep the recycle bin with just a little storage for emergency. This is a simplistic way of explaining how we get overweight and obese by excess calories, carbohydrates, and fats and also why it is so easy to become overweight and so hard to lose weight.

Diet

Now that you have an organized plan, the next step is implementation. Eat regular meals (breakfast, lunch, and dinner) and snack less. You can cut junk food slowly until you no longer feel the need to have it. You should train your mind to resist the temptation of junk food. Remember that the work of the liver and kidney is filtering the blood and eliminating toxins from food and junk. The more junk you eat, the more work the internal organs will have to do. Use common sense: if your body rejects them but you like them, who has priority here? Not you! But if you feel that you must have junk food, fine. Have it in smaller quantities. After all, you are dieting to be healthier, more fit, and happier, not the other way around.

Follow the same strategy with beverages. Reduce the amount of unhealthy beverages, and increase water quantity. If you don't drink water, now is time to start. Don't kill yourself trying to drink the recommended eight glasses per day; just make sure you are drinking a lot of water. Do you know that the human body is 80 percent water? We use it every second, and we must replenish. Do you like to have kidney stones? Then drink water. If you crave sodas and can't live without them, drink fewer and not so often. Switching to diet sodas is good in terms of calories—zero calories—but you still get the other junk in it, especially Coca-Cola. Sprite and ginger ale are better choices, but ask your dietician or search online to know more about what is good and bad for you.

If you hate to cook, now is the time to change that attitude and win double—you make your own meals and learn cooking skills. There are numerous cookbooks, online recipes, and TV programs to help you learn. Start with simple dishes and move on up as you wish. In no time, you will love to cook, and you will know how to prepare foods that will not make you fat.

For the purpose of your nutrition, you must select meals not too different from your food culture. Say you grew up on pizza, macaroni and cheese, steak, pasta, roast beef, cheeseburgers, tacos, and all kinds of processed food. Switching all at once to rice and beans, potatoes, cabbage, beans, fried eggs, fish, steak, yucca, bananas, and so on could sicken you. To avoid that and still have the diet you need, consult you dietician or doctor before you change your nutrition regimen, or go slowly on your nutritional changes.

Don't fall for weight-loss gimmicks, like dietary tea. It will sure make you lose weight, but it is unhealthy.

Vitamins

When I finished fourth grade in Cape Verde, I was to attend a new school that was three miles from my home. We didn't have a school bus, but walking about three miles to school was nothing! Two years went by, and I graduated from junior high, which was a huge accomplishment. I became one of the few educated kids in the neighborhood. Most of my friends weren't able to make it to fourth grade. So obviously, I was making a distinction for myself among my friends and earning admiration from adults, but I was not satisfied with my achievement. I always dreamed bigger. I wanted to continue my studies. High school was in the capital city. My grandfather, who had raised me since I was two, had promised me to do all he could to support my education. He kept his promise, but we were getting to a dead end. So I had to stay home, hanging with friends and doing stupid things, causing trouble and running away from trouble. That quickly became boring. I started to see my life on a dead end. My grandpa was doing his best to honor his promise, but he was frustrated. I decide to take some action.

I don't remember how I got the cash to pay for the transportation, but I made it to the city. I was very happy to find one of my grandpa's friends, Johnquin, working as a manager at a large retail store in the city. I had hoped he could help me, but he said he was living at a hotel close by, so he could not help me with a place to live. I had visualized my high school world as a paradise. My dreams were growing bigger every day, and I just couldn't wait to start. Now, that reality had whipped me unmercifully. I had no idea about the fate of my destiny. I had never felt so wet and cold in a tropical island on the west coast of Africa as I did when Johnquin said, "Sorry, I can't help."

Sensitive and emotional as I am, I still don't know how I did not break down in tears. I remember my mixed feelings of anxiety, aggravation, and anger. I saw all windows of opportunity closing on me. All that was there for me was disappointment and a sad trip back home. I definitely should have burst into tears right in front of him.

I talked to nobody about my failed venture. Now that my slick move had turned into failure, the next thing would be explaining to my grandfather why I did what I had done. I worried over how I would continue my education, as well as worrying about my grandfather's anger when he found out. I was having nightmares about it. My grandfather, however, was very understanding, and he told me not to worry and that he would find ways for me to continue my education. And he did.

As much as it hurt him, he swallowed his pride and asked his daughter, my godmother, with whom he did not get along, to offer me a place to stay. She resisted initially but then accepted. Maybe she realized she was doing me a favor, not her father.

And so the school years began, and things started out fine. I was mocked by some of the students, but farm students always get mocked by city kids until they loosen up and go with the flow. In no time, I had friends from the country and the city. My grades were not outstanding but were enough to move me on to the next term.

Things started to shift to bad at home. My godmother became increasingly annoying and gave me a hard time over any little thing I did wrong. I couldn't hang around with my friends, never mind fooling around with girls. She was cooking one kind of meal every day for weeks, cooking something a little bit different, and then returning to the previous menu. Vitamin supplements would have been welcome! She was giving me hell, so I would not return the next year. And I didn't. My family understood her game and agreed that the following year, I would not go back to her.

I got mad at my situation and decided to make miracles happen. Books and notebooks became my best friends. When I got tired of studying at home, I would grab my studying materials and go someplace where the government had stopped people from progressing with their clandestine house construction. Most houses were half done, and all of them were roofless. I would find one that was quiet and clean, making sure it was free of human waste, and I would study subject after subject. Out of anger, I got addicted to studying.

At the end of second term, my grades were something to turn heads; at the end of the school year, I was one of the best. My math teacher couldn't believe that I beat his best student. Out of about thirty-six of us from the countryside, most had quit by second term. I was one of the six who made it to the next grade. I returned home as a hero.

As you can see, the lack of proper nutrition and vitamins didn't stop me from becoming one of the elite. If I can do it, anybody can do it. When I got to the United States, where you find vitamins even in water, vitamins didn't make me a genius. But the truth is that some people need vitamins, others don't. The question is, who are they? To know the answer, we need to return to how we get overweight and obese.

I believe we get overweight and obese by eating too much good food, too much bad food, or not enough good food. Rich people have money to afford good food. They eat too much of it and don't exercise. That means rich people probably don't need vitamins. Middle class, falling fast to the poverty line and below, can't afford good food 100 percent of the time. Junk food is part of the groceries. They should include vitamin supplements in their nutrition. Poor people, who can only afford junk food and a little bit of good food, definitely need vitamin supplements.

Some people are not inclined to take vitamins because they feel the industry is not truthful about the ingredients in vitamins. There are others who rely on vitamins instead of good food, because animals and birds are given steroids and fed junk that will pass to us through meat, milk, and eggs. Farming is toxic from pesticides and all kinds of deadly chemicals that will sicken us by eating fruits, vegetables, and other crops.

Nutritionally, I believe that smart choice is making sure of what we need and taking care of what we need. We cannot rely on the purity of products alone, because we don't have what it takes to distribute pure food. Actually, we have complicated nutrition so much that there doesn't seem to be enough natural food for all of us. So we need to learn to live with junk and other bad stuff out there, which unfortunately will get worse in terms of quantity and quality. We live in a tricky world, getting trickier every day. We need cool minds to figure things out and move along. Finding out if you need vitamin supplements should be an important consideration for your well-being. And it comes down to this: you need, you take; you don't need, you don't take.

In health, fitness and balanced nutrition help us go a long way. And vitamins should not be left out of the equation.

Diet Awareness

Assuming that you decided to do the right thing for your health, be aware of the obstacles on your route and understand the sacrifice you need to make. Those who give up on dieting and exercise didn't understand the sacrifice, didn't prepare for the challenges of the journey, and became stressed out and frustrated and returned to their comfort zone.

Take your time to get organized and ready to start. Don't begin your diet and exercise program until you are sure that you will reach your goals. If the reality of your life doesn't allow for you to start now, stay busy on getting ready to start strong. A strong start means that you take the necessary time to make sure that you have reachable goals. It also means that you understand that it won't be easy, but you know that things will get better as your body, mind, and spirit adjust to your new reality.

There is also a "smart start"—you can start your diet and exercise for a month or two to try it and then have a real start.

No matter how your start begins, you could come to the point where you will need to slow down, so the adjustment of your body, mind, and spirit is not torturous or pushing you to quit. If that happens, just slow down and keep moving. A smooth path lies ahead. It's much like flying for the first time. When the jet takes off, you might be nervous or unsure, but when it levels off at cruising altitude, you enjoy the ride. If the captain finds a little turbulence, turns around, takes you back to the airport, and your flight is canceled, wouldn't you be angry? Everyone would. The captain uses his experience and preparedness to make appropriate adjustments and proceed with the flight plan.

The same thing happens with almost every journey toward any goal in life. Now, here's a tip that I want you to take to heart: when you start your diet and exercise, picture yourself driving on a long dead-end street. Whenever you feel like returning home, remind yourself that there is no U-turn—and step on it!

Fitness and Nutrition

Some fitness processes speed up metabolism, and metabolism wakes up your appetite. Some experts suggest replenishing your muscle with protein half an hour after you work out. (Protein shakes are handy. Tuna fish, egg whites, and meat are the best sources.) Only a balanced diet will bring the best results in fitness and nutrition. Working out hard but eating badly is a bad combination. You will harm your system or even get sick. Fitness and nutrition are the two main ingredients responsible for keeping you healthy and energetic. They are the foundation of your health and happiness.

Whatever the reason for being overweight, fight it for all the good reasons. Use the resources available to you to change your nutritional life, keep the change in your pocket, and enjoy the thrills of life. From the extra cash, donate some to food pantries and other organizations aiming to feed the hungry.

It's a good idea to keep a small chart that shows the number of pounds you want to lose weekly. Get a scale and weigh yourself in your birthday suit first thing in the morning on an empty stomach. On your chart, write the day, month, and year that you will reach your goal. That is your most important celebration date. Look at it every morning and every night to stay focused on the new you that is waiting for you. It has been done before; it can be done again. The only difference is that this time, you are doing it. Call all your friends, especially those who supported you, to celebrate the new you with you. (Don't forget me!) Post the new you—happy, sexy, slim, and fit—on Facebook and let others be jealous of you. Let's get this war on obesity started!

17

Relationships

The circle of life is funny. When you are a kid, you can't wait to grow up. When you are an adult, you wish you were a kid again. When you are single, you want a relationship. When you have a relationship, you want to be single again. You hear people say things like, "Marriage is good, but single is better"; "If guardian angels protect us from catastrophic events, where were they on my wedding day?"; "Everything changes after the marriage"; and my favorite one, "Why buy the cow if you can get the milk for free?"

A relationship lives with us. A relationship defines us. A relationship gives us the meaning of life. A relationship gives us the opportunity to leave the seeds of continuity after we are gone. A relationship is this is it, especially when it lives with true love.

I am sure that life has taught you that every good has a bad behind it, and every bad has an ugly behind it. Let me remind you of the amusement of your kids and the thrills of sex almost anytime, just to mention a few. The bad behind those things, which usually comes years later, includes the stupid fights and senseless arguments, jealousy, anger, and loss of freedom, just to mention a few. And the ugly comes when somebody is caught cheating. Stress, depression, and anxiety take over, and the ship is in trouble.

True Love

True love comes from the magic. It is the one that drives your heart insane, makes you lose weight and sleep, changes your moods and behavior, throws your emotions off, and forces you to act dorky. Some of us call it love at first sight. It is more likely to happen in your teens, as our potential to fall in love and to love and be loved is at the highest level then. Here, nothing matters but the power of the emotion, chosen and expressed through your heart. Color, race, beauty, and all other things we consider before falling in love matter not when we deal with true love. Whatever that power is, which sometimes we don't understand, our sight sees only the best of that person, and we want nobody else for company. And it is painful too.

If you have a true love, with God's blessing, you could be tying the knot in a few years with your high school sweetheart. What a beautiful thing that is! You should appreciate it, and keep its flame glowing. Unfortunately, not all of us have the luxury of tying the knot to our true love. Instead, we are left with the hard work of searching for somebody to love.

In your late twenties, assuming that you have done your job right, you have gone many places, seen different faces, and accumulated enough knowledge about the good, bad, and ugly of relationships that you are ready to engage in any commitment and make it work. And if you have a love-at-first-sight for company, you are truly blessed! From here, things will only get better! You see, true love usually comes with lots of beauty and personality, for the most part, which eliminates the work and time spent on collecting personal information to make a plan for a smooth relationship.

But nothing is granted without some work. I would like to tell those who are lucky to be in this relationship to work at it for the sake of love and the gift from God. Use your head to stay ahead of the game, and keep the flames glowing strong. And the rest of us, the unlucky ones, are left with the hard work of searching for somebody to love.

Searching and Personality Research

After living in the fast lane for a while, there comes time to settle down and to begin to live the American dream, show your friends that you can do it, and show the world what you have in your hands. Whatever your reasons, be sure that you do the work before you say "I do." The homework is the search for the right person. And on this search, personality research is on the top of the homework list. You could start with a family tree. A family tree can tell a lot about the person standing in front of you. Sometimes there is not even the need for research. Say you found that your lover has numerous brothers and sisters and cousins, but only a couple of them get along. Isn't that enough clue to the kind of family it is? But most of the time, you need to dig deep in your search.

Before you start searching for the true personality of the person you are involved with, you should know all you can about yourself. Your homework is not an easy task. You need maturity to help explore an individual's characteristics—the older you are, the better are the chances of getting a clue to someone's true personality.

Here's one thing in life that I don't understand: sexual power and desire are mismatched. Male sexuality is said to peak at age eighteen, while for females, it's thirty-five. At eighteen guys are hard like a rock and can go on forever, but they know nothing about what they're doing. From that point, there is an increase in their experience, not sexual power. There will even be times that Johnny will refuse to get up and party (what an embarrassment!). But fortunately, guys enjoy sex more as they take more time exploring it and focusing on doing it right. They use sexual wisdom to compensate for the loss of hardiness and quickness in getting ready for another round. Females' sexual power and desire go up as they age. At about thirty-five, they reach their sexual peak; they can't get enough of the stuff. And guys want to provide but are unable to cover the demand.

Why didn't the Creator allow men and women to get their sexual peaks at the same age?

When you reach your mid-twenties, it's time to take things seriously. Our personalities don't exist by chance. They are the fusion of chromosomes, genes, and other complicated things from our parents and our adventures during our first five years. They all come to play in the game that gives us distinctive characteristics. These characteristics, when carefully analyzed, come close to what we really are; some physical clues are very close to the true personality. Boys wearing baggy pants, in love with hoodies even in hot weather, walking slowly and almost never smiling are one of a kind. And physically unattractive females who don't socialize and almost never find anything amusing are generally troublesome. We blame media for emphasizing beauty, but the truth is that people with great personalities and who are successful are mostly beautiful. If you were born beautiful, you have a head start on the road to success. If you were born not physically attractive, you have some catching up to do. If you want success, you have to create it. Take measures to upgrade yourself with the support of higher education and appropriate fashion, and change what destiny gave you into something special and desirable. You have great potential hidden inside you—bring it out. It will give your personality a new look and a different path for success.

During the search and research of personality, you have to worry about things such as traumas caused by sexual abuse, rape, oppressed childhood, or tragic family death. They should deserve the most attention because they show negative effects in adulthood. Children raised under stress, oppression, and in an abusive environment have hatred lurking under their skin. When they mature or take control of their lives, they will unleash the evil within, unless they had a chance to replace traumas of the past with happy memories.

Culture, tradition, and philosophical principles can be problematic in adulthood too. Mothers often pass along their philosophical principles—negative or positive—to their children. You may find it offensive if she stands up for what she believes in, but it will be up to you to take her daughter's hand in marriage or take a hike and save yourself from trouble.

After you have enough information in personality research from a distance, get more information close and personal through open dialogue about life experience. Using open dialogue to discover your lover's true personality works better when both of you understand the need for this. It must be clear that this is not about revealing each other's dark past but something important for the future of both of you. And if anything seems left out on purpose, leave it as it is. You could be touching matters too sensitive to share.

After the dialogue, you should move on with your independent secret investigation. Rely on people and friends for valuable history, but make sure that your questions don't raise suspicion. You don't want your lover to think that after an honest conversation, you've gone behind his or her back to dig trash. Carefully, do whatever it takes to turn over all the stones. By the way, understanding your lover's circle of friends is another important clue to the kind of person your love is and will be. Once you have enough information, sit down alone in a quiet room, shut all your emotions down, and objectively analyze your information. The answers to lots of questions should be obvious. For example, after getting angry out of the blue so many times, you have figured out what triggers mood swings or bad behavior—it has an explanation in the drama of the past. If you end up confused in your analysis, ask for help from people you trust.

You may say we are the new generation. We move from one relationship to another and go through divorce after divorce. We don't have time to waste on this kind of research. Besides, we are conditioned to let our feelings and emotions guide the destiny of our relationships, beginning by letting the heart choose. Maybe that's what is normal, natural, cultural, and appropriate now. The younger we are, the more normal this sounds, which allows me to tell you that young adults shouldn't bother with extensive personality research, because age doesn't help to jump over feelings, emotions, and tricks of passion to get to a realistic conclusion. I also don't think that it is a good idea for anybody in their early twenties to get seriously involved in a relationship.

The greatest benefit of researching your lover of good intention is that when you have the score of your homework, you will have the necessary information to make smart decisions about your future. And if you choose to end the relationship, you will not face big surprises, because you knew where you were heading and what to expect.

Personality is one of the essential parts of all relationships. The lack of it drives relationships to a sudden death, followed by a complete failure. Forget the first-sight love crush and all the bullshit of the new generation. In fact, the new generation is worse. We have tons of social problems caused by broken families, beginning with kids suffering emotional stress from being raised by single parents. So use your mind and resources to find the road that will easily take you to where you want to go with your relationship, instead of taking the road that everybody's taking. Keep in mind that if you want to have the best, you must have it from the best. To have the best, you must find the best. The best is in the personality first.

When you know who you are, you know who your lover is, and you love each other, the foundation of your relationship is tornado-proof. But this gift very seldom drops from the sky.

Choosing

Men and women have different tastes and opinions on what is beautiful or attractive. Whether based on physical attributes or an emotional connection, there is enough variety to fulfill the diversity of taste and preference. In some cultures, it's still common practice for parents to choose mates for their offspring. I call it the game of royalty—they may impose principles with which sons and daughters disagree. In India, this culture is taken so seriously that in extreme cases, relatives murder their own for marrying someone not approved by the families. These days the most common and simplistic way to an arranged relationship is through blind dates—way simpler, way less stressful. You like what you see and you go on another date. You don't like what you see, and you never meet again.

But your parents are not completely wrong. They can see things for the future than an eighteen-year-old doesn't see, and they know that you could easily make a big mistake at that age. And so, they step in to take charge before your inexperience strikes tragically. They also want the best for your future and the protection of culture, tradition, and philosophical views and family reputation, including economic situation. At the same time, your parents are not completely right either. It is true that parents know better in this case; they have been there and done it. They know what you don't, and you might never know what they know, but this is about you first. What about love? When the relationship is prearranged by families, and the lovers accept it for the sake of family tradition, it will not last. Any relationship based on something other than love, trust, and commitment heads toward chaos and separation. In fact, even when all these rule, separations do happen for some reason. This is your game and your battle. Your parents should stay on the bench and give advice when you ask. You have the right to marry the person you love, not the one you're forced to marry. So tell your parents to back off and empower yourself to get better than what they could give you to marry.

Assuming that you have found someone with more than 50 percent of the qualifications to be your lover, your next move should be getting rid of the dilemma. For example, just because your lover has some minor issues doesn't mean you should forget him or her. Understand that there is work to be done from both of you. He or she is what your heart has chosen. If you feel confident about the future together, there's no listening to people, friends, or family. Go for your dreams and turn them into reality.

We all want to choose the most beautiful or handsome person, and we want to accept what our hearts have chosen for us. But unlike personality, beauty and looks are easily manageable, and love is complicated. We can improve upon physical appearance, but love is a blind driver without license and registration. My mom used to remind us that love doesn't go to the table—that means that love is not food. Actually, if you love him or her, do some serious thinking for decision making now, not after you hate him or her because the true personality has come out as a real asshole or a slick bitch. Don't follow your heart without regard to other qualities needed for the relationship. Changing someone's character could take a lifetime, and it will be full of stressful battles.

Life has no guarantees. You could have done the best possible homework in choosing the right person and ended up with the worst imaginable person, but if you don't choose the right one, you increase the odds against you. On the other hand, don't keep backing up to the end of the line because you must find the right one. Usually when our lover has a bad reputation, we ignore it or don't give attention to it because nobody is perfect. We are in love, and though love is blind, we have not used a guide dog, so we think that whatever is causing pain and suffering will go away with time. The reality is that when we begin a relationship, the train of chaos starts its engine, and we could be on the journey to hell for years to come.

Let's come down to common sense: grab one good apple from the basket and go home. A good apple has to be the one that your heart has chosen. You have inspected it and found no signs of bugs. It could be the poorest and ugliest apple in the basket in the eyes of the world's standards, but you don't care, because you know that was the apple with the most of your prerequisites.

Once upon a time, a smart guy from the islands was married to a rural girl of much lower social class. He liked to go to the square on Fridays after work to hang with his friends and coworkers. The square was surrounded by tall buildings, with one long avenue running north/south and a long rotary that connected the avenue to the east side, with many pockets of relaxation spots with iron chairs. Right in the middle of the square was a statue of a man and a woman with a baby on her lap. My grandfather explained that the statue was of a doctor who had saved the life of a mother and her child, although both were meant to die in labor. The statue stood ten feet high and had a fountain that gushed from five surrounding wells. It was a beautiful view during the day, and very spectacular at night under the light of many streetlights, adding something magical to the square at night.

This paradise was the main social encounter place where you met relatives, friends, strangers, and single people available for a relationship. On Sundays, between six and ten o'clock, this was the place of the main event in town. This was the place to close the evening.

His friends sat in front of the Department of Justice building to kill time after an eight-hour shift. They usually gossiped about intriguing girls in town, discussed internal politics, and argued about other countries' politics and sport teams. As he approached the bench where his friends were gathered, the conversation died, and suddenly everybody was uncomfortably quiet. "You don't need to stop because you see me. I heard you. I know and I don't care."

"Victor, don't get mad," one of his friends said, "but your wife is so ugly."

"I know. That's why I married her. So you guys don't look at her. I come home to find food on the table, my clothes are ironed, I have no jealousy, and we don't fight. She knows that she's ugly and nobody wants her. She's happy to be with me, and I am fine with her."

The most important thing in this game is finding the one that meets more than 50 percent of your needs and desires. That is the right choice for you, because you are choosing for you, not for your family, friends, or the world. Once you have chosen the right one for you, when it comes to the necessary work and diligence to make relationships work, you are ahead of the game.

Your Family

Like many other animals, we are creatures of community. We all became members of one clan or gang at some point, and we called it family. Then the family tree came with its uncountable branches, so we can all fit where we belong. To this day, isolated individuals are considered antisocial or abnormal. And it became our duty to ensure the continuity of the family tree.

Individuals' needs and desires, as well as the environment and socio-economics, play a big role in building a family. Financial considerations play a role here too, because providing for the family's basic needs—house, food, and clothing, up to education and luxuries—is a big financial responsibility. Economic changes have caused couples to have second thoughts about family size. In the country, the average family size was eight kids; now it's dropped to three to four and one to two in suburban areas.

As the crops become less productive and poorly surviving, technology reduces the need for human bodies in agriculture, and there's the difficulty of finding and keeping a job with good pay for a variety of reasons. Population control encourages couples to have fewer kids, and the pinches of economic stress and commitment to the job or business all affect the timing and size of family. There are numerous issues out there that frighten us from even thinking about building a family.

You may spend years living with your parents and never having responsibilities, but by your late teens, survival needs and social pressure kicks in, and it all comes down to having a family of your own. There is also the need for a soul mate. Some individuals couldn't care less about the family tree continuation, cultural tradition, or anything related to marriage, but they care about their survival and sexual satisfaction. And so the steps of committed relationships and family begin. The next step, then, will be finding the perfect person. In reality, however, there is no perfect one, but there is the perfect one. Let me explain: the perfect one doesn't exist; you build it.

When you have a lover that you consider perfect, you will fool yourself into thinking that you are all set. You stop looking for signs of imperfection. You stop worrying. You just enjoy the good times—until you start cursing and want to kill somebody. But when you work with what you have and both of you are happy, you have turned an imperfect gift of destiny into a desire of your desires. That is your perfect one, because he or she is the right one for you. One thing that you need to take into consideration is that there's work—sometimes hard work—to be done in finding the right person with whom to start a family. Whomever you end up with, he or she will fall into one of the following categories: the Right Gone Wrong, Reckless Selection, No One Bothered to Pick Up the Pieces, Victim of Circumstance, or Match and Mismatch.

The Right One Gone Wrong

All relationships are meant to go through rough times. That's just part of the fun, part of the game. You could be one of those lucky ones who was raised in a family where unkind words were never spoken. Wonderful! But the truth is that your parents were very smart to choose the right time to settle sensitive issues so you didn't grow up in a stressful home environment and get the wrong impression of relationships. As you grow, however, you begin to see fights between loved ones everywhere you go. And then comes the drive to experiment with a relationship of your own. You go through hard times, and you can't understand what is going on, because people who love each other should live peacefully. Unfortunately, relationships don't move like that, no matter if you have the right one or not.

Now, when you are blessed in a relationship, you have lots of good things that many couples don't have. That could mean less work to maintain a wonderful relationship—with ups and downs, of course—but if you close your eyes, shut your ears, and cross your arms, your relationship will suffer the consequences, because you didn't do any work to protect your treasure.

Reckless Selection

When you don't select the best players, your team will suffer. Reckless selection will definitely get you in trouble. This type of union is just about sexual satisfaction and other conveniences never based on love. At some point, someone else will come along, and separation will take place. So, if you are fooling around with risky sexual behavior, don't let things reach a serious level. You start out on the soft ground of sandy beaches. You may never find the strength to move to solid ground. Protect yourself, enjoy the time, and look for companionship somewhere. Change your approach, and start from scratch, making sure that what you have could turn into a good relationship. You see, anything you do recklessly brings trouble and sets you up for consequences that leave you with a sour taste in your mouth and a lifetime of regret. Luck could be on your side at the right time, at the right place, and could change the odds for you—or even turn your biggest mistakes into fabulous results. But do not count on luck to bring you the greatness of a strong relationship. You can be certain that reckless selection will, one day, leave you stranded with a broken heart.

No One Bothered to Pick Up the Pieces

This is translated as a death wish to each other. Both are sleeping back-to-back, with a space enough to cuddle an elephant in between. Dialogue is reduced to minimum or zero. No one wants to take responsibility for the ship, the river is left to run its course, and a ship crashes right around the corner.

There are times when this kind of journey should be left to die, but there is time also when it should be saved. You decide where you stand and do the right thing. If the relationship has to die, make sure you have done everything in your power not to pull the plug, and once it is dead, you will not mourn or try to revive it.

Victim of Circumstance

A bad breakup without possibility of reconciliation is one of the most common circumstances by which we are sucked into victim-of-circumstance relationships. Both you and your former partner have wished death on each other, or hopes of burning in hell, or prison time. The split is forever—definitely forever! The closest bar is now the hangout paradise, as the goal is getting hooked up fast with someone new to forget the past. Ironically, the first comer is someone looking for the same refuge. And because life is a bitch, it doesn't give the best when you need it the most. The bar closes; you take the first person available. The next morning, you wake up with a horrible situation in your lap and a pounding headache. You look for the ingredients to make your favorite hangover remedy or just rush yourself home with a guilty conscience.

After your head clears, you try to remember what happened. Don't blame yourself for being stupid. Instead, get your act together to figure a smart way out. Give anger and pain the necessary time to go away, and then—only then—start a fresh relationship game. This time, make sure that you use your head and put yourself ahead of the game. Play safe, play smart, and protect your score.

Susana was the fifth child of the eight siblings. She grew up under the watchful eyes of her parents, brothers, and sisters. At eighteen, she had finished school and began working in a government facility as a clerk. This new step in life meant freedom to date without having to hide from brothers or answer questions at home. She was in charge of her destiny. Beautiful and full of desire to explore the wild side, it was just a matter of time before her life took a turn. She was patiently waiting for the right guy to come her way but she couldn't wait forever.

One of her coworkers, a man in his early thirties, was attracted to Susana. The age difference was one minor obstacle for her, but his physical appearance was the major one. At least in Susana's eyes, he was unattractive, with zero chance to score with her. He knew that his game had to be tight, but experience was on his side. He knew that Susana was single, in need of a boyfriend, and could fall easily. So his strategy was to crush her with attention every day, eliminating other competition. One summer afternoon, with an abundance of love in the air, after everybody had gone home, a dark corner of the building where they both worked was about to witness the end of something special and the beginning of something terrific. The fear of being caught rushed their time together, but it was still enough time to celebrate pleasure with love and passion.

Nine months later, she gave birth to her first son. The father was the man she thought was too old to date and too ugly to take her virginity. Her family couldn't understand what had happened to her, and they left no room for the relationship to go on. Susana, who couldn't support herself 100 percent, lost the love of her father and the respect of her brothers and sisters. She had a rough road ahead. Susana's story tells us that even when we dislike someone, when brushed by daily contact, it can turn, with time, into serious passion and intimacy. Coworkers are the most dangerous hunters. If both of you are single, a one-night stand can happen, passion can kick in, and trouble begins. Be aware of what destiny throws at you, and stay firm on shooting for the best in order not to fall into a bad place by being a victim of circumstance.

Match

It is most beneficial for a relationship to be with someone from your culture and tradition. Food, clothing, behavior, philosophy, and other aspects of life are familiar to both of you. When you are sure about your final choice, even if this person does belong to your culture, tradition, and everything else, please do your homework before things become serious. The head start that you have here should not stop you from making your choice of someone from a different race or culture. But in either case, respect tradition and culture as much as you can and have one approach for your union. It is your new life. You have to mold it strong enough to withstand the storms that will come later—guaranteed.

Mismatch

You could be an illiterate person, but a miracle could happen, and you could be in a relationship with someone of high class. Here, love offsets the difference in point of view about everything. As love fades away with time, disagreement will replace the happiness that love brings, and an inferiority complex will take over to ruin things. Any simple disagreement could become a big argument fueled by negative and derisive comments. This gap of education and life experience will bring a higher level of jealousy and complicate the circle of friendship, even when all else falls into place. Say you are a construction worker married to a corporate manager. You will not fit in at gala parties, business trips, meetings, after-hours conferences, and so on, and that will spark thoughts of infidelity. An inferiority complex could trigger a fight, and you end up losing the battle and the war.

The lack of education can put a huge dent in people's ability to succeed financially, which in turn doesn't help with financial obligation in the household. And that would be the smallest problem on the way.

This kind of relationship is not common, and I don't think you should dream of one, but if you are in one and want to stay in it, know that work is at least double when there is a huge education gap.

Raising Your Family

Everybody has an idea of the number of children they want to raise, based on tradition, culture, and socio-economic and environmental conditions. Assuming that you have done your homework, which puts you ahead of the game, you have nothing to fear. Things will fall into place with ease. The homework consists of finding the person closest to your standards, sitting down together to talk about things, and agreeing to raise the family to the best of your ability, putting the health and happiness of the family first and personal desires second. You are able to maintain a house in a nice neighborhood, with separate rooms for boys and girls. Your income comes from your small business or good employment, and you have plan B on standby in case you lose your current income. You have savings to cover your full expenses for at least six months, and you're debt-free and your credit is good. You already decided where to live so your family will be a distance away and the families and the in-laws will stay out of your business. I think you are ready to take the big step.

You may think this sounds too perfect, and if you wait for a "perfect" situation like this, you will never raise a family. Well, you're wrong. And get this: those who believe in it have raised kids who are good citizens, on their way to becoming famous business people, lawyers, doctors, or celebrities, and they may run for the presidency of the United States. And there is less chance for their kids being with kids from broken families on the streets, with their destiny in the hands of uncertainty and cursing their parents. Smart people with big dreams and the right mind-set for their families wait until they are ready. The relationship will stand on firm ground.

But this is not the only way to raise a successful family. In fact, having "perfect" conditions doesn't guarantee perfect results. Anybody with a positive attitude and clear vision of a decent family, based on morals, respect, and perseverance, will raise a family as good as the one raised under "perfect" conditions. Commitment, serious work, and a continuous struggle to stay on course is necessary for raising a family of any kind.

The first three years of a child's life is the most interesting and enjoyable to almost any family. Just weeks after birth, the baby starts to show signs of health and normalcy, and we are fascinated watching a child's brain development. The curiosity kicks in, and the child does things on his own, such as picking up a piece of paper on the floor and bringing it to the trash bin. We help by giving him another piece of paper to "put it in the trash," pointing our finger to where the trash bin is. We watch him walk to the trash bin to dump the paper. He then goes to the kitchen to grab a spoon, but the drawer is too high. He comes to ask you for help, but you don't know exactly what he wants, except that he needs help. You get up to follow him and realize he might want a spoon. He nods his head when you ask him if that's what he wants. Then he pushes the power button to start the TV and then the microwave. He can communicate his desires, even though he can only say a few words clearly. There is a whole world of happiness that words can't describe during those first few years of children's development.

There's also the impaired child who brings happiness in a more unique way and raises your love and determination to give all the happiness that he deserves. Everything he does correctly brings joy to your heart; every one of his smiles hits you straight in the heart and lights up the flames of happiness, bringing tears of joy.

Then, at about age five, things take the rough road. Depending on the child's temper and how stress-free the family is, the ride can be a little bit bumpy. The child begins to challenge your decisions, has tantrums, and exhibits annoying behavior. The child ignores your "stop" commands until he gets a spanking or sent to time-out. There are arguments over taking a bath, going to bed, getting up, and turning off the games. Then the child turns thirteen and makes you wonder if he's really your child. That's when you show how good or bad of a parent you can be. I suggest that you learn all that you can about the teenage years by reading books and talking to counselors, pediatricians, and psychologists, because you will need all the help you can get.

Puberty is responsible for all devilish teen behavior. Girls want to dress pretty to walk through the mall every day, shopping and showing off for boys. Boys want to walk through the mall to check out girls, cruise around town, and hang out on basketball courts and baseball fields. Both genders want to go parties, come home late, text all night long, experiment with sex, and have fun.

You, as a parent, don't have the resources to beat the devil—teenagers— but if you raise your child right from the very beginning, when the teenage years come, the clash will not be tormenting, because moral conduct that grew with the child will help smooth the edges of miscommunication between parents and teens. Respect, communication, and understanding between parents and the teen will pay off.

Some parents over-monitor teenagers' activities and give little room to play and experiment. The guidance comes down as demands, which is not acceptable to teenagers going through their rebellious phase. Parents will face challenging times when the teenage years arrive, no matter what. One of the biggest helps you can have is education.

Education doesn't eliminate the hard times that teens will face. What it does is give a way for teenagers to have a breakthrough and a good chain reaction. Education gives parents a boost in living the American dream and beyond. Their kids will have many productive ways to escape or deal with difficulties, which are brought on by biological changes that they cannot control. They stay busy as they search for ways to make their dreams come true. For example, they could be consumed by sports in school, or they could be highly involved in music or acting or any other activity that promises a bright future. By the time they finish high school, they already know what the next step is. If they don't know, they won't focus on going back to school, and they will have too much free time to do nothing. Kids without direction often get into trouble, begin to build criminal records, and have a dim future.

But there is one approach that seems applicable to all parents when dealing with teenagers: give teenagers the space they need. Times may have changed since you were a teenager, but the reality stayed the same. By giving teenagers the space they need, I mean you need to ride along with your teenager's changes, be open to questions, and offer opinions based on the experience you had when you were a teenager. You'll need to replace the word *don't* with the words, *I think you shouldn't.* You let your teen ride on higher ground while you, now on lower ground, watch and give guidance carefully, if needed. The teen will respond with love and appreciation. There could still be misunderstanding and anger but of short duration only. In the end, both you and your teen will benefit from a great relationship, hugely helped by education or its power.

Boy or Girl, Which One Gives More Headaches

Socially speaking, girls are more difficult than boys in their teens. Girls go through greater hormonal and emotional changes, which in turn bring higher levels of stress. They need more supervision than boys do. Girls can easily get messed up, become pregnant, and see their future going to waste. Parents have the burden of raising the grandchild. Also, there is the molding and protection of character for girls, which is the responsibility of their parents. The supervision of girls is more stressful for parents.

Of course, there are exceptions to the rules, but the bottom line is this: your job is to make the transition through the teen years easier. Even when you seem to run out of patience or ideas, avoid getting to the breaking point and making matters worse than what they already are. When you don't have anything nice or helpful to say, say nothing. Your sweetheart has turned into a devil right in front of your nose, disrespecting you and everybody in the family. Don't offer your head for sacrifice, but don't put the gloves on either. Teens fear nothing. You play hard, they play harder; you play rough, they play rougher; you push them to the ropes, they throw you out of the ring. But if you play nice, they calm down.

The irony is that while teens need you desperately now, they will push you away harder than ever. You, as a parent, have the responsibility to do whatever it takes to guide them, to lead from the heart with a cool head and fresh ideas, and to do whatever necessary to make this very delicate transition of your kid's life easier. Now is not the time to impose house rules, such as "As long you live under my roof, you will do as I say." Now more than ever, you need to pick and choose your battles carefully, and ask for help when you are not sure.

The Devilish Triplets: Trust, Jealousy, and Cheating

Trust is one of the hardest things in any relationship, because too much trust is bad, not enough trust is worse, no trust at all is the worst, and the right amount of trust is impossible. So many things contribute to mistrust. Personality is one of them. Some individuals have a natural untrustworthy personality, which makes them incapable of fighting temptation and pushes them to commit a sin at the first available opportunity. We can see this trait of personality in teens who steal, not because they need what they steal but because of the addiction to stealing. They see something accessible; they take it. They can be caught and punished, but when the next opportunity comes along, they steal again.

Philosophical principles in combination with experience come next in the game of trust. Some of us are raised under strict moral conduct and philosophical principles, where stealing is forbidden, lying is not tolerated, and cheating is unforgivable. Others are raised to do whatever it takes to survive, with disregard to the well-being of others. Parents pass these principles to their children, and these principles become their way of life, turning them into cheaters for life instead of honorable citizens. The sneaky ways we learn in our childhood grow with us, and it seems that survival instinct doesn't let us trust others. There's no denying the fact that good liars in childhood become lying experts as adults. And whatever values we grew up with, we bring into relationships.

We are fascinated with women in a sneaky world. The tears, swearing, emotion, and hurtfulness for our not believing in them are all part of the strategy to cover their suspicious actions and make us trust them.

One of my friends, a genius in seducing women, told me that it's impossible for him to believe and trust women. He knows all their tricks for cheating and making men believe they are not cheating. He said that he will never be happy in any relationship. And I am sure that some women feel the same about men, if men have lied to them or used intimidation, threats to leave, apologies, flowers, or romance as part of their cover-up strategy. Both men and women have strategies to cover their dirty works.

Now, regardless of what you have read, heard, or seen, trust is an important ingredient in all relationships. Too much or too little is not important, as long it exists. And keep in mind that trusting your love doesn't mean wiping out the possibilities for cheating. In fact, when you trust, keep it to yourself, or you can be on the way to a nasty surprise. Trust helps the relationship sail smoother when hard times hit, and it can be a strong cheating repellant. It can be a stinging statement too: "How could you do that to me? I trusted you!" Those words, said at the right time, can cause lifetime injury.

Jealousy

Jealousy is invincible and immortal. Every time we look in the rearview mirror, we see endless moments of jealousy. We fear losing our love to someone lurking somewhere. If we had the confidence that when we lost our love, we would move on, get a better love, and forget the past, jealousy would stay away from our hearts. But that's not the case. The madness of fear takes over, giving us jealousy as a weapon to protect what we have, instead of the confidence to live fearless. In affairs of the heart and sex, jealousy lives right next door.

Some of us are crazy-stupid jealous. Despite the awareness of its bad consequences to our health and relationships, we don't change our behavior. In fact, some of us see jealousy as a good thing. Oh yes! Many men and women think that their lovers don't love them unless they show a high level of jealousy. Humans are complicated! Smart couples define grounds of restricted behavior to avoid mistaking simple behavior for actions that trigger jealousy.

Cheating

A man might follow his soul mate; check her pocketbook, e-mail and voice mail; set up hidden cameras and tape recorders; call work randomly to see if she's there; ask her coworkers and friends for insights; ask the kids who Mom talks to when he isn't home; not allow conversations with any man at all; and promise severe punishment if he even hears rumors.

He doesn't realize that if she's about to cheat on him, it's not his control-freak techniques, threats, and intimidating behavior that will stop her. He makes her feel like a bird in the cage, so she will fly away at the first opportunity and cheat on him as revenge for her loss of freedom. The authoritarian, macho attitude, combined with control-freak behavior will never work. Worst of all, he may be cheating on her, yet he will show increased jealousy and lack of trust in her, just to cover his own acts. One day, he may come home early from work to find a stranger in his bed.

The Signs of It

Regardless of the motives, there are always clues that someone is cheating or is about to cheat:

Behavior change: Your love returns from work not as enthusiastic as usual and heads straight to the shower. He or she is irritable around you; starts frequent arguments over simple things; has a lack of interest in conversations or doing things together; increases activities with friends out of town; and comes home angry with excuses that don't make sense. This one could actually mean that the cheating has been going on for a while, and it's getting serious.

Sneak phone calls: Frequently, the phone rings, and it's someone asking for a name you don't recognize. Or when you answer the phone, the caller hangs up. The caller didn't talk because he or she wanted to talk to your love, not you.

Social changes: Suddenly your lover is dressing nicer, wearing fragrance and cologne, visiting the salon more often, criticizing your wardrobe, and so on. These are all signs of something fishy.

Emotional slow-down: The romance has diminished, sex is not as frequent and enjoyable, and excuses such as "I have headache. My stomach hurts. I am tired. I am not in the mood" become the daily sex repellent.

All these and many other actions are indications of cheating behavior. Watch for them so you can take action, but before you act, make sure you are right, since there are many other things involved in our daily activities that make us show cheating signs, while in reality, we are as faithful as we can be.

Consequences

We have carried the belief for a long time that a woman must be submissive and faithful to her man, while a man can get away with almost anything. Many cultures allow men to have many women, but society is always harder on female cheaters. It sees cheating as a huge bloodstain on an expensive white dress, and a bird's poop on a man's hat. I think this is one of the cases when fair is not fair. And to make matters worse, cheating almost never goes under the radar forever.

As long as all the actions are kept classified, no one gets hurt. But when spies discover your stash of secrets, or when you fall short on your promises, chaos is unleashed. If you happened to be in an abusive relationship, and your spouse is famous for cheating on you and demands that you do nothing about it, it's almost certain that society will understand your situation, feel your pain, and grant you forgiveness. On the other hand, if you are treated like a princess and honored with faithfulness, society will stone you to death.

The closer to home the cheating happened or is happening, the harder it will be to bring understanding. For example, cheating on your lover with a stranger on a getaway or vacation is not as deadly as cheating with your lover's brother, sister, or best friend.

Also, the older you are, the more deeply involved you are, and the longer the time invested in a relationship, the more devastating the consequences of cheating will be. In your teens, you can fool around with as many boys and girls as you find available and get away with it with just a slap, black eye, or a temporary loss of relationship, and it will all be good by next week. But when you invest fifteen years in a committed relationship, with kids, school loans, and joint assets, cheating could be spelled as a .35 caliber between the eyes and a lifetime trauma for the kids, who will live without parents—one buried, another in prison for life or waiting for the death penalty.

Understanding Cheating

Cheating is part of what we are. It has evolved with us. The survival instinct and urge to satisfy our needs drive us to take measures that sometimes are not approved of by others. I also think that men have a higher drive to look for opportunities to cheat. From both sides, there are those whose cheating is understandable and those that are just a cheap shot. Some of them have sexual desires that are impossible to satisfy with one partner. They do their best to preserve the integrity and hold the need until the boiling point, and then they surrender to whoever is handy. It's sad and unfortunate that they can't be faithful no matter what they do. They are what they are. They might want to hang on faithfully to the relationship but can't, because their condition doesn't allow them to, and soon trouble is unleashed.

The second class of cheaters is the players. They have no immediate need to cheat, but they always choose not to back down when they meet an easy prey. This behavior starts in high school, where many students don't graduate because instead of staying in school and studying, they are chasing fun and sex. After getting it, they move on to the next prey. Then there are the crimes they commit because circumstances allow it. They resist, but invincible temptation comes to break our personal moral conduct and principles and allow wrong to happen.

When I was twenty-seven, I was a full-time housekeeper at South Shore Hospital in South Weymouth, Massachusetts. A group of high school students was working in the same department as I was, and we would chat with each other. One day, one of them told us about her guilty feeling. She and a bunch of friends went to Canada on a weekend getaway. Everybody was having fun and going wild with booze, sex, and rock and roll. She was the only one holding back, out of respect to her boyfriend back home, but at some point, liquor took over. Her thinking wasn't clear anymore, and she fell flat and easy, and the rest is history.

You see, she tried her best not to cheat, but she got caught up by circumstances that made it impossible not to do what everybody was doing.

But cheating needs a blessing when it's right and luck when it's wrong. Many years ago, a friend of mine came home from work and noticed that his girlfriend's car wasn't in the driveway. When he went in the house, he called for her to make sure she wasn't in the house. When he was sure he was alone, he lay down on the couch and called a woman. The conversation went from sweet to sweeter, from "What are you wearing?" and "I can't wait to see you" to descriptions of how he would "give it to" her the next time. Like magic, his girlfriend jumped up from behind the couch, screaming and shouting accusations. She had caught him, and there was no way to deny it.

By the standards of many people, cheating should be punished. If you need an extra piece of pie outside your territory, you could be in trouble already. You can try to make your partner understand your needs and ask for some room to play. I don't know what you will get for answers. I know it depends on many factors such as seriousness of the goals of your relationship, your financial situation, culture, religion, tradition, and most important of all, your beliefs and approach to life.

By my standards and principles, if cheating brings you higher happiness, makes you a better person, puts you on the higher ground and ahead of the game without hurting anybody, then cheating should be granted to you.

Any serious relationship touched by the evilness of cheating has sensitive issues to deal with, but "if there's a will, there's a way." Terminating a relationship due to cheating could be a bad decision. That doesn't mean, though, that you should force yourself to stay if the other party is not willing to work things out. It would be foolish. It is almost guaranteed that you will go through hell and endless fights, kids will be raised under a bad family environment, and everybody will lose. So pack, leave space, and select what will be best for the ones you care about the most; it's the only choice left.

Use your head and your cool to understand the circumstances of the cheating, instead of using your rage, emotions, and vengeance as a generator to process your thoughts. If you want to work things out and stay in the relationship, let me remind you of "forgiven but not forgotten"! Don't stay with the idea of forgive and forget, because it will not work. We have what it takes to forgive but never forget. It could make the relationship stronger after both agree to forgive. Give forgiveness, and don't worry about forgetting, because you won't ever forget. We are humans. We came with software to store a large quantity of memories. They are not erased by pretension and desires. So handle the facts after the fact. It's almost guaranteed that you will find new ways to get things back on track.

Handling the Devil

When you drive a used car with high mileage, and you neglect small repairs, you can count on facing major repairs, as at some point, problems will need repair. To avoid headaches, you repair it before the problem gets out of hand and costs you three times more.

Periodic maintenance—oil change, engine tune-ups, tire rotation, or monitoring fluid levels, for example—are as important as doing repairs on time. Taking care of those things ensures that your car is reliable, long lasting, and in good condition for selling or trade-in.

A new car gives you a break, but you know that you must take care of basic things so you don't get headaches too soon.

A relationship is no different. Disagreements left in the air will decay the relationship. When we take care of small disagreements in a timely and peaceful fashion, the best of the best wins. That doesn't mean disagreements will not come back, however, but it is wise to take care of the relationship.

Couples have big lists of things to take care of to avoid disaster. One of the top items on the list should be sex. Sex is like this: if we have to, we'll go to war for it. It's a major drive of all relationships. Without it, the relationship has no chance of survival. Sex maintenance is the priority of all priorities, but many of us don't know, don't care, or care insufficiently. So let's clear the air a little bit, beginning with quantity verses quality.

Quantity means nothing if quality is poor. In fact, poor quality reduces the quantity down to zero.

Guys, it's not how many times you can smack it, how long you keep it rock solid, or the size of your Johnny that matters. What matters is how well you do what you are supposed to do. When your partner doesn't want to do it, watch out. It could be the sign that the quality is diminishing the quantity. Even when there's love and passion in a relationship, if sex is poor and old-fashioned, it will lose its excitement. Getting it only once in a while is also as good as dead. What you want to do is prioritize quality. Once you do that, the quantity will find its way, and you will never go hungry again.

There are tons of things we can do to keep sex as alive and exciting as it is meant to be. Some are unique, but most of them apply to almost everybody. The best medicine is getting your imagination running wild. Every time you imagine something new, try it out. Motel, movies, casinos, parks, the beach, a countryside trip, skating, skiing, flowers and gifts every now and then, and vacations, are just a few good things you bring into the maintenance of your relationship. Then there's the magic trick—what only the two of you know: the favored positions, touch, words, ornaments of the surrounding space, oiling, kinky, and so on. Never leave your magic tricks behind. And when you run out, ask and tell. Read as many erotic books as you can, especially the Kama Sutra; watch adult videos; and do whatever is safe and healthy to keep things warm under the sheets.

The Mystery

If you've already found the G-spot, don't lose it. Stay in touch at all times. If you haven't, don't feel bad. And don't be confused; they say that when you find it, you'll know that you've found it. But what it brings could be misleading. Your girl could be having more than usual excitement, letting you think that she's truly riding in the wild side by the power of the G-spot. Sometimes the magic has nothing to do with the G-spot.

We already know that we are equal but not the same; we all carry our own sexual uniqueness, so enjoy what you have within your reach, and keep looking for ways to improve it. It is our sexual uniqueness that makes some of us enjoy sex quietly, while others enjoy it aggressively. There are also the ones who lie there and let you do your thing but deeply enjoy every bit of it. Some like it rough all the time; others like it just interesting; and some go with the flow. If you're talkative, be careful not to call out the wrong name. And to women, men like the talking, moaning, groaning, and screaming, but please, don't overdo it. They know when you are faking the joy and orgasms. Be real.

The Power of Education

Education, society, economy, and success are all in one tight relationship. Talk about a chain reaction!

When you hold the certificate of higher education, you hold the power to get a decent job. Your social life is great as you hang around with people aiming for a brighter future. Your circle of friends includes people focused on solving problems, instead of creating them. You hold high standards, and you guide your actions according to your standards. You practice what you preach. You get yourself a matching partner for a relationship, and you build a nice family, raising kids to be good citizens with potential to achieve higher goals than yours. You win, society wins, and you did your part to make this world a better place.

When your financial world is the same as the one in a Third World country, your life is a struggle in misery. If you are a high school dropout and can't handle landscaping or construction, manufacturing will not welcome you either. There aren't many places you can earn some cash. If you are an uneducated girl, your options are not any better, and the chances are that you'll have a baby and go on welfare. Since you don't have a higher education, you should see yourself living a messed-up life in ignorance and poverty. If you marry someone for financial security, you will live in eternal hell, as love, passion, and care will die, your spouse will drive you crazy, and life will never be a pretty thing again. Your troubles will double. You might be in and out of jail on charges of domestic violence. When time comes that you want to clean up the mess and ride a different path by getting a job, your criminal record and lack of education will prevent you from finding employment.

You must take into consideration that we need economic power and money to survive, including in relationships. Education is the best tool to help you.

Education in Communication

When you're educated, you have the power to direct your life, control your behavior, observe and listen to your partner, and convey your point of view in a way that brings understanding and compromise. You learn to think before you act, and you forgive others for their mistakes and wrongdoing. You plan, implement, and control your life. When disagreement is unavoidable in public, you hold your argument until you get home. You dream of a prosperous future for you and your family, and you ensure that your kids have a better life than yours. You fight to maintain integrity and physical fitness to better participate in issues that aim for the welfare of your family and others around you. You know when to swallow your pride and dreams for the sake of your family. You feel special. You don't get angry, because you place yourself on higher ground. But above all, you have the power to communicate; you have clean fuel for relationships.

The power of communication helps to keep sanity in your relationships. You use your higher education or great personality to organize your thoughts and direct your arguments to understanding, instead of displaying ignorance, stupidity, and an inferiority complex to subdue the viewpoints of others.

No Education and Laying Low

When people have low or no education, their point of view on life is archaic or dominated by an inferiority complex. The man will fight for dominance, and the woman will refuse to be submissive. There will always be a clash with regard to who's in charge. Jealousy surfaces and is bad for the relationship. Both parties want to know where the other is and what the other is doing at all times. Mistrust becomes a common factor in your relationship—he questions her phone calls; she is suspicious of other women he talks to at parties. It is impossible to have peace and harmony in a relationship of this kind. Everywhere you turn, there is hell brought on by your own ignorance and stupidity. It's like you have a ticking time bomb strapped to your chest—how can you not explode?

The Split/Breakups

There are times when both of you commit to put your best efforts to work—all cards have been laid out, all advice and recommendations have been followed—but the ship still rocks through rough waters without the clear possibility of smooth sailing anytime soon. Continuing the journey under these circumstances would be foolish. Splitting up becomes the only smart decision.

In this case, if there is no compromise, the anguish, stress, and anxiety will fade away after the emotional storm quiets down. If you had someone almost available, you can try taking things one step forward. If you had a secret lover, the secret lover now becomes the number one. If neither of these situations applies to you, then you have to look for someone else to love; not a big deal.

If there is a child involved, things won't be easy. The innocent child should not suffer because your relationship with your partner—the child's parent—ended. That's painful and heartbreaking enough. Be the parents that you are supposed to be. You must maintain contact with your ex for the sake of your kids. Put your children's welfare on the priority list. You will be proud of yourselves, and the guilt of not being there for your children will not haunt you. That's how the split should be done. I applaud those parents. This is what I call intelligent work of individuals, whose wisdom allowed them to go the extra mile to do the right thing, even if that meant swallowing their pride.

The other kind of split is the one that benefits no one. Battles can happen on any given day; the relationship is falling apart but no one bothers to pick up the pieces. The parents don't give a damn about the welfare of their children. It is war and revenge at full force, twenty-four/seven. There may be acts of violence perpetrated against property, such as slashed tires, busted windshields, or smashed windows. There could be phone harassment and public embarrassment. The husband or wife may need to get a restraining order against the spouse, although that may do no good. It's like going from the frying pan and into the fire—and taking your kids with you, the innocent souls who are victims of their parents' stupidity. Eventually, children will finally let their anger and frustration take over them because of their parents' behavior. This kind of separation is one of the ugliest ones. Usually, the partners have a low level of education or act as if they do. I believe that most legal separations begin with filing the divorce papers and splitting the assets. After the fight between lawyers, the court settles it. Child support is set, alimony support is set, custody and visits with the kids are set, and divorce papers are signed. The split is official, and the legal system takes over to ensure the compliance. In most of the cases the ex goes home as light as a feather, thrilled to be free again.

Divorce between people with a higher level of education also includes papers to sign, but the partners often will stay friends, at least for the sake of the kids. It can be a nightmare when the court sets the child-support amount, and the legal system takes over to ensure compliance. The system works well, however, in ensuring that the support is given according to the court's ruling. When alimony is settled by the court, the father is slapped on both cheeks—he doesn't even need to turn the other cheek. Child support starts right away. Alimony could start when requested. It's reasonable to set alimony if the ex is in need. Some women, however, refuse alimony at the time of divorce settlement, but any time that they feel in financial distress, they can go back to court and request alimony, as long the ex-husband is alive. I think that it is wise to look into the laws of marriage and divorce and have a clear idea of what comes attached to marriage, before you tie the knot.

Breakups are no fun. Instead of celebrating freedom, we cry and seek revenge. The person who chooses to end the relationship suffers less stress than the partner, as the one who leaves usually has someone lined up as a replacement or looks forward to being single again for a while. The one who is left behind, however, feels rejected and incompetent. He or she might beg for reconciliation and for answers on what caused the breakup.

There's not a quick fix for any breakup. Depending on the length and depth of the relationship, it can take six months to years to get over it, and the memories—good and bad—will never vanish completely. If you are the one who left for someone better than what you had, good for you. I just hope you've done your homework, and you know what you're doing. Where I come from, in this type of situation, people will warn you to make sure you are not dismounting the horse to ride a donkey.

And if you are the one who was left, the forsaken incompetent, don't play stupid. It's impossible not to feel the pain, but don't do what everybody does by running into the arms of the first person who comes your way. Give some time for the pain to ease a little bit; bring some confidence to your body, mind, and spirit; and live again. When you were tied up, you wished for freedom, didn't you? Well, there you have it. Date as much as you can, and take that as preparation for your next serious commitment. Celebrate the new you; enjoy every bit of it for as long you can. Take commitments out of the equation, and focus on one-night stands and casual encounters. While you are having fun, watch your finances and protect your integrity.

If you don't think you measure up, don't use your financial power to cover for whatever you don't have. Just use what you have to your best ability, and be aware of false orgasms and compliments. Some girls play to never lose. They will date you as long as you promise a fancy evening. Even if you don't measure up in her eyes, your cash could earn you another date or two, but that would be as far as your cash could take you. Beware.

Don't be cheap, but don't spend more than you need to spend. When you encounter a gold digger, pull out nice and easy, and shut the doors and windows to avoid future entries. Raise your socio-economic status as high as you can, earn yourself a better job, and then hang out with your match.

Things you can do to protect your integrity include avoiding being caught in a compromising situation with regard to sexual encounters. If you are accused of rape, even if the sex was consensual, destiny will spin your life in a wild court ride. Even if you can prove the truth, many people will never believe it. If you're convicted, you will face time behind bars. Never take it for granted that what happened to other people won't happen to you. This kind of attitude walks you right to sour surprises. Use your head!

You can do good things while you enjoy the good side of breakups, including working up your credit to the best it can be; empowering yourself with higher education, which gives you the tools to get a good job, own a small business, and earn a second income; feeling economically independent; or buying a house. If you can't cook, clean, do laundry, shop, or iron your clothes, now is the time to learn, so you can live independently. Live it, get used to it, love it, and set your mind on the possibility of living like that for the rest of your life, not rushing things. As long you are able to take care of yourself and are having plenty of sex, don't settle until you are sure that you have found someone closest to what you want, and you are ready to handle whatever comes. As long as you do your homework, you should never encounter rough waters that you can't cross safely.

Reconciliation

It doesn't matter how tragic or painful the breakup is, time heals the wounds and negative thoughts fade away. At that point, one will miss the other, or the two will miss each other. If neither person has done well since the separation, there's a possibility of reconciliation.

Reconciliation is a wonderful thing, and it's even better when kids are involved. If you can't read the happiness in their faces, just ask them; they will tell you. Everybody wins big. But when you stay separated for seven or eight years, with constant fights of all kinds, and you end up with an ugly divorce, it's probably too late for a reconciliation.

Secrets to Second and Last

When you are young, you have time to deal with many breakups, which is good, because you learn something new with each breakup.

Relationships may last from three to twelve months. But as we grow, so do our emotions. Jealousy now is an adult. Breakups are troublesome at times and painful most of the time. We must become responsible now and respect life. We are tired of little games, and when we tie the knot for good, we think that we are done with breakups—until we find ourselves single again.

For whatever reasons, after time heals the wounds, you might want to be in a relationship again. We are humans, social beings with families. Women may think men are all the same, and men probably think the same of women, but we are unique. The problem is that we have so many things in common. It is no surprise, then, that we can finish a relationship with one person and go through the same hell with a different person. To avoid that—another crash and burn—you must make it last forever this time. To do that, work from your experiences, good and bad, from previous relationships.

If you happen to remarry your ex, you must make it last forever. Breaking up a second time when kids are involved is a crime punishable by the devil. That's guaranteed. So return for good or stay away forever. Your kids don't want you to reopen the wounds you gave them.

I believe that God created us to enjoy life, to reproduce and fill the world. And for those who believe that our Creator is not God, I am sure they still agree that all living species became social creatures that reproduce and form families, and that being in a relationship is part of what we are. Trying to escape that reality is like running from the essence of life. So it's our obligation to find a relationship and maintain it in good spirit, take what it has to offer, and give it what is expected and needed.

Maintenance of a relationship relies on many secrets and obvious techniques. It is our duty to find each one in our relationship and work at them. I think that one of the best remedies for relationship maintenance is knowing what destroys relationships and then guarding against that. The next best remedy is counseling, before things get out of hand. Stay ahead of the game. Give trust, keep jealousy under control, and use your brain to deal with relationships.

Investing in relationship maintenance is reinforcing the foundation and support beams of "happily ever after." The amount of work, money, and stress is discouraging, but the outcome is priceless, with lots of great sex, strong love, and passion in the package to help us enjoy life and fill the world.

18

Stress Management

STRESS TAKES AWAY OUR POWER to succeed and the desire to live, and it brings all sorts of health complications. It also gets us in a lot of trouble, physically and emotionally.

Our experiences make us realize that life has incomprehensible phenomena. When you are late to work, a doctor's appointment, a job interview, or picking up the kids, all sorts of things you don't need will occur: the traffic will be heavy and slow; you will hit all traffic lights on red; there will be road construction and detours; other drivers will cut you off and then slow down once they're in front of you; or you'll get stuck behind a school bus that makes stops at each house on the block.

When we are stressed, facing the realities of life will not make our day go by easily. As a matter of fact, when we're stressed and pressed for time, it seems we're more likely to get pulled over and fined for a minor traffic violation, get in a car accident, or get a flat tire far from home. The irony of life and our stressful mind team up to destroy us.

Right now your state of mind might be troubled. There's too much stress, frustration, deception, lack of enthusiasm, and temptation to do something outrageously stupid. Life is just beating you down unmercifully. The relationship between mind, body, and spirit has been run down by a truck. Everywhere you turn, there's disaster. You just can't hold yourself together. And the worst part of it is that stressors are everywhere, dumping their loads on you, from the time we're teenagers—if not earlier—until death. There is no way to escape stress, and if it reaches an unhealthy level, it throws you into hell and makes life lose its meaning. It even can kill you. Some of the health complications it can cause include:

- *Heart disease.* Stressed-out people have a higher risk of high blood pressure and other heart problems. Stress might have a direct impact on the heart and blood vessels, and it can make you reach for the wrong things to put out the flame—drinking and smoking. So many people blame stress for their smoking addiction, which in turn will cause more health problems.
- *Asthma.* Studies show that stress can worsen asthma.
- *Obesity.* Stress causes higher levels of cortisol, increasing the amount of fat in your belly.
- *Diabetes.* Stress can worsen diabetes in two ways: First, it could increase the chances of unhealthy behaviors, such as getting hooked on unhealthy food. Second, stress seems to increase the glucose level in people with type 2 diabetes.
- *Headaches.* Stress is considered one of the most common triggers for headaches and migraines.
- *Depression and anxiety.* Stress is connected to depression and anxiety.
- *Ulcers.* Stress has a negative effect on ulcers.
- *Alzheimer's disease.* Research shows that stress has the potential to speed up the progression of the disease.

To avoid stress-related complications, use a cool head to find out the root of the problem and take care of it. Sometimes you bring stress on yourself—for example, you spend your rent money on drinks with your buddies—but sometimes it's through no fault of your own, such as a job layoff, a death in the family, or other health complications. You can't stop them from dumping stress on you. All you can do is cope with the situation, let time ease the pain, and figure out strategies to fight the stress.

I am going to offer a few steps to keep your stress levels under control, but it is your obligation to implement them and to discover other ways to help:

- Put your personality awareness to work. Once you are aware of others' personalities, you can avoid situations that will lead to confrontation.
- Avoid negative energy. Avoid friends and places carrying negative energy. When everything goes wrong in your life, it's better not to seek advice from your buddies who happen to be as stressed out as you are. Places of negative energy aren't just funeral homes and graveyards. The street where your unkind English teacher or that annoying bully live is filled with negative energy. Avoid walking or driving there. A better choice is seeking help from your buddies on higher ground. They could even have been in your place and have advice coming from experience. You will feel empowered to go home and fight the stress.
- Comforting expressions of sympathy may be helpful. It makes you tell yourself that "this too shall pass," but in reality, it keeps your head buried in the sand. Do something to control your stress.
- Track it down. When you don't know where you're going, you won't know when you get there. The same theory applies to stress management. You need to know the amount of stress you can handle and keep yourself in check. Some people can handle tremendous amounts of stress, while others can be miserable with just a little. When you understand your stress level, it will be easier for you to control it. Stress is tricky. You could be doing something that seems to keep your body, mind, and spirit balanced, but you're actually increasing your stress. For example, playing video games can be fun and entertaining, but being a loser all the time definitely increases your stress level.

- Obey the laws, rules, and regulations. Doing so saves you court time and fees, as well as time off work to settle disputes in courts.
- Beat the rush. Leave home ten to fifteen minutes early in good weather and even earlier in bad weather conditions. Being late increases stress, so you need to allow for possible accidents, road construction or any kind of traffic jam, and inconsiderate drivers on the road.
- Get your finances in order.
- Avoid arguments that increase your stress level. Don't put on your sparring gear; just prepare yourself to lay low.
- Soothe your body, mind, and spirit. Read books, watch comedy, go to clubs to dance all night, visit your friends, go to the park, see a movie, celebrate holidays, invite friends over—whatever it takes to soothe your body, mind, and spirit.
- You must have your chain of life running smoothly in order to have a life of balanced stress. Each broken section of the chain brings its own amount of stress. How you are affected depends on how stressed you already are, how many broken sections you have, and how important they are—unemployment, loss of a family member, and breakups and divorces are the killers. Give priority to your chain reaction as the foundation for your stress management.
- Laughter, sex, and exercise is important. Each one alone is a powerful weapon to fight stress. Combined, they become a stress vest. Don't let them stray from your sight—ever.
- Stay ahead of the game. When you are ahead of the game, your stress level is as low as it can be. Stressors can come from every corner of life and dump on you, but if you stay ahead of the game, you won't be affected.

It would be wrong to assume that when you have money—a lot of it—you have no stress. The more money and assets you have, the greater the amount of stress, as your stressors are diversified and more powerful. Not enough money gives you stress, but too much money gives you stress as well. What saves the wealthy from exploding is their capacity to handle the stress and stressors. They are worried when they have no stress. I think they realize that no matter who you are, you just can't live stress-free, and they also realize that their lifestyle is stressful in itself.

Rich or poor, don't let stress take the best of you. Understand its connection to your life, and do your best to keep it at healthy levels at all times. Staying ahead of the game is the best cure for anyone.

19

Retirement

On one of those nights when my grandfather was in a good mood to tell stories, he told me about a man whose father was old and getting ill. Things got complicated and eventually, the man couldn't take care of his father anymore. One night he took him to a large cave in the mountain, miles away from home. When the man was about to leave, his father asked him for a knife. "Why do you need a knife?" the man asked.

His father replied, "It's for cutting the blanket in half."

"Don't cut the blanket," the man said. "You'll need the whole blanket."

His father said, "I'm going to give you half for when you get old too."

Tears filled the corners of the man's eyes and blurred his vision. He clenched his lips to resist crying out in pain. He carried his father back home and loved him forever more.

That story has stuck with me all these years. I imagine that the man had to go through much harder times in taking care of his father, possibly more than he had expected. I just hope that he took the experience as a lesson to prepare for his retirement in a way that his kids wouldn't have to go through what he did. And I think that reminds us of some of our responsibilities to our parents.

As youngsters, we don't want to hear about retirement. We don't even know if we are going to see tomorrow, let alone retirement that seems millions of miles and ages away. We have confidence that somehow we will hit it big, and the retirement will be taken care of. Besides, who has time to waste on retirement planning and worries?

The reality is that retirement is so important that the government, at some point, realized that it would be a wise move to have employees do mandatory savings for retirement, and it created many programs to help you when you retire. Most governments have this plan in place.

If you don't have any retirement savings, your last days could come full of disappointment and frustration. There's a little break with the help of daughters and sons, but that also comes with lots of stress and headaches.

We enjoy our journey in life, and then we give space for others to live. It is expected that we will leave this world a better place than it was when we inherited it. Throughout this journey, we face different stretches of road. The first is the one where we are receiving care, tools, and instruction to use them to move to the next stretch of the road, where we will be behind the wheel, putting to work what we have learned and improving our skills to survive independently. Here is where the fun resides. It's our responsibility to indulge in all the goodies life has for us, reproduce for the continuity of the family tree, make our dreams come true, and continue to have more fun. The last stretch is the beginning of the end of the party. Here, we should take care of ourselves by ourselves, but we take all the help we can get, because this last stretch of the road is bumpy and gets bumpier with each new turn. The party is not over yet, but it has taken a turn to fight for fun and survival. Ironically, the fight becomes more ferocious while we become weaker. This unfriendly road of retirement is what cries for most of our care before we ride on it.

Life in retirement consists of two distinct realities: one is what we bring with us—our personality, philosophy, education, and experience—and the other is what we will find there—the ecosystem, the movements of society, and the technology. Each one has its independent powers. Combined, they make our retirement less rough or more bumpy. Here is an example of how they work collectively in our retirement: you could belong to a family tree that is humble and smart. Chances are that you will do well in your retirement because your personality alone will help you deal with difficult times and situations. You also have the characteristics that attract people to be willing to give you a hand when you need it the most and even when you don't need it. But if you belong to the family tree that's vengeful, less smart, and lazy, your personality drives people away from you. You are likely to be the most hated tenant in public housing. Your character could push your own family away from you. You might fall and break a leg or have a stroke and have to enter the hospital, and your personality might cause you to curse the medical staff that has been caring for you. Oh yes, personality is a major player in your retirement.

Philosophical principles are about how you picture life and the choices you take to live your life. If you chose to party a lot, drank, smoked, didn't exercise, ate poorly, and worked in hard labor (mining, construction, landscaping, carpentry, etc.) your hard life will make the road to retirement rough; the way you lived your life corresponds to the way you will live in retirement.

Education plays a big role too. The higher your education, the greater the chances of living well and traveling a less rough road later. Experience also is a big indicator of the life you will have in retirement. If you found ways to survive in your early years, you'll find ways to survive in retirement. But if you avoided hard work, never worked your self-esteem, and never were a leader, you have accumulated poor experiences only. They will not help you in your retirement. If your bad temper and criminal inclination forced you to spend most of your time in jail or on probation, and if you never landed a steady, decent job with good pay and benefits, you shouldn't count on your experience to give you a good helping hand in retirement. Also, if you never had a chance to deal with economic intruders and other disturbing elements of life, and the relationship between your brothers and sisters or your kids is not that great, none of these is an experience you should count on. And if you have been divorced a couple of times and the exes are still alive, you could see your retirement money slashed to pay alimony.

The package we bring with us to retirement is pretty heavy. What about the package we will find there? It will be as heavy or heavier, with old realities we couldn't change, such as the economy, society, government, and teenagers, as well as new ones we will not be able to change, such as weather and illnesses. And your strength to accept them will be weak and getting weaker. Your cash will be slashed to cover basic needs and some needs-intruders, especially medical expenses. Chances are that a lot of needs-intruders will be put on hold forever, never mind the wants-intruders. Even when you have a social security pension and other retirement income, you will live on a fixed income, while life expenses go up every day for reasons you can't control. And how will you stand in a bad economy? Well, the chaotic economic world creates a chaotic society almost automatically, with increases in vandalism, home robbery, and attacks on the elderly, among other social malfunctions. You might have to hold that thought of walking around the neighborhood to benefit from the fresh air, exercise, and quietness of late night or under moonlight because those hours could be deadly for you, when desperate teens look for ways to grab some fast cash or release stress through violent acts. You could be a victim of circumstance.

There's also less politeness and desire to help citizens, as everybody is frustrated and stressed out from one thing or another.

If government is all screwed up in a good economy, it is clear that in a bad economy it will be dead. Its responsibilities increase, and it must find ways to respond. Unfortunately, cutting expenses is always one of the strategies to restore order, and social services take the hardest blow. That means help for those in need, including retirees, will be less, and patients' participation in health care costs will increase. You will have a hard time with your co-pays, but you will get less help and be asked to pay more.

Legacy

In your retirement, it's time for you to enjoy the rest of your life. It's not the time to hassle yourself to finish the third story of your house that took you a lifetime to build. The savings that you have should go to you, not to material things that will not do you any good after you are gone, and you know that your time can come at any time—really any time. But that doesn't mean you should waste your money to make sure you are using all of it because you can't take it with you. No, that's wrong.

It's wrong also for you to worry about not leaving a legacy for your family, which is considered by many people and cultures as proof that you did well in life. You could suffer and go through hell to protect your after-death reputation. That's really stupid. Use all your pennies to take care of yourself, and prepare your soul to enter heaven and paradise. The world will forget the good things you did and remember forever that one big bad thing you did. The wealthy are the ones able to leave wealth behind. When they do, they will not get the credit, because people will say that whatever they left behind didn't belong to them, that it belonged to the poor people the wealthy stole from. If you have enough money on which to live and still leave it for others, then by all means do so. The world needs it. Otherwise, live every bit of your life, and forget how you'll be seen after you're dead. Even if you grew up in a culture that values one's life based on what is left for others, break free from that ideology. If you want to be remembered after you're dead, give your kids and family an education and the tools to take their destiny in their own hands, so they don't have to rely on your legacy and government favors to get by. As a matter of fact, giving your kids an education is an assurance of their survival after you are gone. Also, a debt-free situation is one of the biggest legacies you can leave for them. You don't leave them with thousands of dollars in health costs and a family feud to deal with.

It's your duty to have a good life of your own, which includes your economic freedom all the way to the end. If you do that, chances are that you will have your house paid off, and your bank account could have a few hundred thousand by the time you retire, and you can still find something you like to do to keep you busy, and possibly earn some cash to add to your retirement expenses. And when you see the day approaching, split what you can't take with you to those you care about by writing a will.

Everybody gets what you leave them, and they'll appreciate it. If you have to consume everything before you go, then so be it; you will still be dearly missed forever.

I am trying to support myself until I die. If I reach my goal of becoming rich, I will leave some for my children to share. The best inheritance I can leave them, however, is what they are getting now—education and advice on how to take care of themselves. The oldest one needs a little more work to kill what seems to be a curse of getting in trouble with the law, but I have confidence that he will get back on track. The second one has his certification in auto mechanics, the dream of his life. He plans to own a garage. The third one is lost in the world of rap, hoping to hit it big someday. His strategy scares me a bit, and I am sure that he needs to shuffle the deck to get better cards. But he has his high school diploma, so I have faith that he will bounce back to reality in case rap doesn't cut it for him. The youngest got his first-degree junior black belt in martial arts at the age of nine. He's now in eighth grade and is an honor-roll student and has been taking acting classes for a few years.

I am not thinking about their welfare only. I have intentions to use the power of their education for my retirement, in case I happen to need a helping hand. You see, when my son gets a garage, I could ask for a housekeeper position or to be his advisor on how to handle customers. I am sure my son would find something I could do for pay. I have the same game plan with regard to the other three sons. I wish God had given me a daughter too. I would move in with her to ensure there was some order and respect in the house.

I will not go through any pain or sacrifice in my retirement by leaving material things to keep my name alive. If that is what it takes, my name will be dead way before I die.

Should You Rely on Your Daughters and Sons?

If your kids got an education, followed your guidance, and settled just fine, they will not take you to a nursing home. They will help you with rent, car insurance, and other expenses that you may have, or they may even demand that you come to live with them. If you hadn't been there for your kids when they needed you the most, they would have ended up as high school dropouts, with records with the law and struggling with life. On the other hand, they could have good intentions about helping you in your retirement, but the reality of their lives might not give room to help you much. The world economic condition has been harsh on everybody. Taking care of themselves might be a struggle, never mind their parents.

Even when your daughters and sons are doing well, the responsibilities of taking care of retired parents are huge, costly, and time-consuming. Your kids, responsible adults now, must stay focused on their responsibilities with respect to their daily activities and plans of their own retirement. Keeping employment—the most important responsibility—comes with its demands of staying sharp by upgrading their skills, and that could include taking night classes or going to seminars, and in some cases a shift of career becomes mandatory. Then, there are family obligations that could include finding good day care, managing the time for drop-offs and pick-ups of the kids, piano lessons, karate classes, soccer practice, basketball practice, football practice, Boys and Girls Clubs and YMCA programs, school conferences, and church and community activities. These things take a big chunk of parents' time, bringing stress, frustration, and bites out of their finances. So where's the time and money to take care of you?

Since someone must take care of you, your daughters and sons will get together to decide how to share the workload.

To the daughters and sons, your parents sacrificed to turn you from golden kids into diamond citizens, expecting that you will take care of them when they can no longer take care of themselves. It's your duty to make sure that they don't die alone, in pain and misery. In most cases your parents will have no life in retirement, you will have no life while you take care of them, and medical bills will keep you broke long after your parents are gone. I am sure you wouldn't like this situation, and you shouldn't expect that your kids will like it either, which makes it important that you take care of your own retirement. Take all the help from your kids, but keep them out of your retirement so they can focus on their own.

Retirement is becoming an increasingly daunting subject for everybody, even to the wealthy. Of course, the best remedy for a retirement to be less troublesome is money. It will stop a lot of pain, all the way to your last day, but retirement is capable of having pain and suffering that money cannot stop. If you are already there, you need to find ways to cope with what you have and make the best of it. It's too late to make big dreams come true. At this point, there isn't much you can do, other than accept the reality with its surprising moments. Find things that you can change, such as your attitude toward life and others around you, and accept what you can't change. Try to be polite and have a positive approach to difficult situations, instead of cursing people and destiny.

To those not there yet but approaching fast, increase the intensity of preparation for when you reach retirement. Start by doing the math and counting your pennies; try to know where you stand at all times. Don't be traumatized by studies suggesting that you will need twenty times more than what you make now so you can retire, but don't ignore the studies either. They come with detailed calculations and could be right. Your retirement could include expenses for surgeries, long hospitalization, or nursing home care to accommodate a disability. The cost for your care could be way beyond a million dollars. Plan for your retirement the best you can, according to your possibilities.

Don't assume that you are ever too young to plan for retirement. You have two distinct choices: one is putting yourself on the path to becoming wealthy and working hard at it. The other is preparing for the journey by consulting financial advisors and other professionals who can give you guidance in savings and all other available options for retirement. I suggest that you work on both of them. Don't simply live for the present without planning for tomorrow or assume you will be fine, like everybody else. That is a philosophy that covers the pain of losers who don't take retirement seriously and see no chance of retiring.

The reason why you can't rely on that attitude is that when you reach retirement, many things will kill your desire to continue to work to support yourself. For example, the government will limit the amount you can earn. You'll have less chance to keep your job for a variety of reasons— hidden age discrimination, for example, or skills that are outdated. Your health also could be an issue. You have no idea of the kinds of health complications that could attack you in your retirement—flu, high blood pressure, joint pain, respiratory problems, diabetes, cancer, Alzheimer's disease, to name a few. You will reach the stage where, in so many cases, your mind says yes, but your body says no. Please take health and fitness as your best helping hand.

20

Game Over

IF THE END OF THE game comes quickly for you, you could take your prizes, your strategies, and your scores with you. But if it lingers, you could go through some storms. Even if you did well in the game, you will have feelings of regret—that's human nature. You will blame yourself, your kids, your friends, and the world for not allowing you to get it all. And it's all for that one score you wanted to make.

If you score poorly, you will be hit by regrets, disappointments, and shame. You will indulge in self-criticism for the fact that you understood the game but didn't play well. We all know the anger, rage, and explosive feelings we have when the game is over and we didn't score well. These feelings are not healthy for you at all. Regardless of your performance in the game, remember all your good memories and travel in your mind to beautiful places. Focus on the enjoyment of the games you played well, and forgive all the cheaters and enemies so you can enjoy the endgame— even though your joints, bones, flesh, and mind will not help you much. Of course, having understood the rules of the game, you might have played smart and lived ahead of the game, earned a name for yourself, and become an inspiration for generations to come. But whatever you have accomplished, the game you are playing now is the one in which you are a winner. So smile, and keep smiling. This is the moment for preparation for the journey of eternity in heaven or paradise. Play the end of the game as relaxed as it can be, and continue to smile more and more. The game … is over.

Afterword

I BELIEVE THAT ONE OF the main reasons for us to hate life is that we don't have a clear understanding of how important we are and how necessary our mission is. We try to discover ourselves and choose the right path, in many cases without ever connecting to life until it's too late. It seems that we don't believe in ourselves, and we don't stand up to the challenges we face, probably because we think that we are weak and meant to fail. In reality, we all count. Some of us count with distinction, others with disgust, but we all are parts of the whole. All of us are part of the complicated assembly line of something extraordinarily amazing called life.

No matter who you are or where you stand, you have come a long way on this journey of life. This first of the three stretches is the hardest. The remaining two are much smoother and easier—part one of staying ahead of the game is all about taking the first step toward a better life. Once you're on that road, things will fall into place, one after another. Yet you can make it harder, rougher, and foggier if you neglect your responsibilities. And so to avoid that, you must watch your step at all times throughout the journey, and if it becomes necessary, change the blueprint that life has given you, so you can walk your path with confidence and reach your goals.

Remember the importance of finances and the chain reaction in your struggle to make life better. A financial mess is one of the reasons why so many catastrophic events with hellish devastation pay us a visit, and lack of money keeps us stressed out and locked in poverty. Almost every goal we have requires some intervention of money, directly or indirectly. That doesn't mean that all we need is financial security to automatically escape the world's daily chaos and madness or to live free of stress, but it certainly is the main generator of a stable life, with great possibilities of making our dreams come true.

For each of us, there is a different chain reaction in life, although it's similar for all. Each of us, however, needs to identify the sections in need of greater attention and take care of them. To some of us, that could be the financial section; to others, it could be the relationship or education section. Do whatever it takes to stay in control of your destiny, but remember that financial security is the main motor of the chain reaction of life.

Now, by having full control of our lives, we will not solve all the problems of the world or wipe the slate clean to start fresh, but we certainly will enjoy life more and make this world a better place. If we cannot treat each other as the brothers and sisters that we are, we must at least come closer and get along better.

In fact, we must find ways to control our lives so that we can guide our behavior away from harming ourselves and others. We can't keep committing atrocities and mass murder of our children and loved ones. We should be fed up with burying our young children, loved ones, and other innocent people, victims of barbaric actions of human insanity. We must take charge of our destiny as the only remedy to cure the pandemic of human barbarity. Murdering our innocent angels must end—and it must end now. There's no race, guns, or illness to blame. There is only the messed-up life we're living.

Having our lives under control means that we have the full sense of our responsibilities. We understand that we are strong and powerful. We have wonderful goals to achieve, and we stay busy doing whatever it takes to put our powers to work. We find new ground to empower our lives, broaden our horizons, and dream bigger. Let's all stand up and respect life by taking charge of our destiny. We can't let anybody do it for us, and we can't wait any longer.

Even though the gap between the wealthy and the poor keeps widening, we are messed up globally, from top to bottom, apparently without any clue about how to do things right. Regardless of our social status and living conditions, we all must keep our heads up, bodies strong, boots strapped, and sleeves rolled up and go to work. Life was never meant to be plain, simple, and enjoyable from beginning to end. It is delightful during the first five to ten years. After that, the difficulties, pain, and suffering increase until the end. But you don't necessarily have to live in pain and suffering.

Life being life—full of surprises from the beginning to the end and beyond—reminds us every day that staying in action and in control and always being ready is the way to go through our daily challenges. Keeping the necessary means to stay in control is ever more dramatic, demanding, and discouraging, but if you do nothing, the matter will only get worse. And so the name of the game is action—determination to continue to act to the last day. To that, add the attitude of accepting nothing but victory in your struggle. Understand that easy doesn't do it, but that you can do it easily. Everything in life comes at a price. Staying ahead of the game has an expensive price tag, but you are rich enough to buy it. If not, you will earn enough. Also, remember that making sacrifices now and getting rewards later is better than suffering forever under fear of failure.

You are about to make changes in your life that will bring criticism from friends, family, and loved ones. Their criticism will not come out of jealousy but because they don't understand your reasons, and they don't see you as a winner. They might ridicule you, and you could lose some of them, but after you reach your goals, they will understand, and you will win them back. You are going to stumble and fall—and fall hard—but you must be smart enough to learn with each stumble and fall. You are going to start your new journey with a firm determination that you will take nothing but victory. Whatever your first goal is, you are going to achieve it, and then set another one and another one until you have a long list of achievements and new dreams. If going through walls and walking on water happens to be what it takes, then that's what it'll take. You will go through hell, but nothing will stop you. You are invincible in pursuing your happiness.

Commitment is now your second best friend—you are your first best friend. Your invincibility principle, as well as your firm commitment, will lead you to read good books for one hour each night, right before bed, to help you stay in touch with your dreams and the means to take you there.

We all are precious and on a special mission. You must turn any nonsense into something powerful, to get you from wherever you might be—stuck or progressing—and to give you the boost you need to go on stronger. Use all the incentive you get from this book and read as many more books as you can find, so you can provide yourself with a continuous link to a power supply for all your engines. Today is the day that you will begin to speed up your process of becoming something much larger than life. You will shape your life for the best and have the determination you need to get you there.

Now that you have begun the new journey, you must stay in daily contact with all the moving parts of your means of commuting. When the pain is unbearable, you are going to slow down, take a deep breath, sit down to give the storm time to pass, and then continue your journey. No one is going to live your dreams for you, and nothing can take away your dreams. You know your traps, your challenges, and your power. You are breaking free and becoming a new you. In fact, as of now, you are a new you. You are not going to let the whips of life bruise you and push you back. First, you are going to dodge the strikes. Second, you are going to wear a special suit. Third, because nothing can stop you, you will take the whipping in order to stay ahead of the game, where you can see yourself as the most valuable player that you are. If you have been ahead of the game, now you will gear up for the game that only you can dominate. If you haven't, now is the time to know how it feels.

You know by now that you count. You are a hero and a champion. And now you are going to go straight to action. The new you will not be just a New Year's resolution. You will check the assembly line of life, lubricate all moving parts, tune up the generator, and get the chain running better than ever—and you will do it today. Your new game has just begun.

And so, until we meet again in *Stay Ahead of the Game, Part II*, keep your game tight and interesting and your assembly line running smoothly. Don't do this because I asked you to do it; do it because you can—and you must.